# The Apocalypse

## A Study in the Book of the Revelation of Jesus Christ

### By Dan Haifley

# Introduction

This book has been compiled with great caution. It has taken many years of preparation and many starts and stops. I am so awed by the book of Revelation that I do not feel worthy to write a commentary. However, due largely to the encouragement of my friends who have patiently endured my constant Revelation discussions, I have attempted to put down on paper some of the things I have learned.

Beginning at a very young age my Father claimed the promise in the third verse of the book which states that reading it would bring a blessing to the reader. So we began night after night reading Revelation as a family one verse at a time. For the first several years we read the book of Revelation once a week and eventually settled into a routine that completed it every three weeks. Those family devotions coupled with my own study and reading have caused me to log well over 1,000 times currently through the book. After nearly 40 years of gospel ministry, I find myself referencing it in almost every sermon I preach.

A simple truth often missed in the study of Revelation is that it is not about a coming catastrophe in the world. The word "Apocalypse" which is transliterated from the original Greek language has been used by movie producers and science fiction writers for many years to present some kind of great end of the world. Massive tragedies are described as "Apocalyptic." Little by little, we have come to accept that this word and the book with its name is about some frightful time in the future that preludes the end of the world. To be sure, the book does reference some pretty scary stuff, but "Apocalypse" doesn't mean "End of the world." The word "αποκαλυψισ" (the Greek word from which we get the word "apocalypse") is translated as "Revelation." It is used in several different ways in the King James Version:

> Luke 2:32 = to lighten
>
> Romans 8:19 = manifestation
>
> I Peter 1:7 = appearing
>
> I Corinthians  1:7 = coming
>
> Every other place (14 x) revealed or revelation

In each case you can see that the word is used to reference a kind of unveiling or illumination of truth.  This fact is critical to the understanding of the book of Revelation.

The "Revelation of Jesus Christ" is not intended to give us dire predictions of the end of the world. It was given to us to describe God's view of Jesus Christ. It is a "Revelation." When taken in complete harmony with the rest of the Bible it becomes the key to understanding many things that were before only alluded to.  It presents Jesus Christ as our advocate and special counsel in heavenly places. It describes the beginning of the church and the end of the world. It also shows us the goal of God in our relationship with Him and the role that Jesus plays in this great saga we call, "Life."

And so we begin the study…...

# Section 1

**Chapter:** One

**Title:** The Divine Perspective

**Summary:** The book of Revelation is written from God's view and must be understood from a heavenly and spiritual perspective.

**Study Outline:**

1.  The Gift of a Father

2.  Truth Hidden from those outside the family

> A. Hidden Truth in Old Testament Prophecies

> B. Hidden Truth in Parables

> C. Hidden from the natural man

3. The Inside view of the Eternal Christ

**1**

# The Divine Perspective

## -The Gift of a Father

The very first line indicates that this book is different from any other:

*"The Revelation of Jesus Christ, which God gave unto him…"*

Take a minute to ponder that line. Stop. Go back and read it again. Just because you know what it says, don't skip over it. It is a most enlightening discovery about the book of Revelation and sets the stage for understanding the whole book.

This is a book written by God, Himself, and given as a gift to His Son, Jesus Christ. As such, it is written from a heavenly view. It is not allegorical or mystical. It is, in fact, actual happenings, albeit happenings that are viewed from Heavens' throne room. It is a view completely unlimited by human perspectives. As Elisha's servant was able to peek behind the veil and see the flaming chariots around him, so John was allowed to see the story of Jesus from the perspective of heavenly sight.

Sometimes that heavenly sight can not be described with human words although John gives his best descriptions. For example: "….they had hair as….their teeth were as….they had tails like unto….etc."

There are things in the book of Revelation thatwe can't properly understand because we can't relate to them in any way. They are written from God's perspective.

## -Truth Hidden from those outside the family

Not everything in Revelation can be explained or understood in our finite state. It is not the only book of the Bible like this. There are many places in the Bible that are difficult to understand. Even the Apostle Peter acknowledged that (II Peter 3:15-16). The truth is there are things written in the scriptures which are not meant to be understood by everyone.

**Hidden truths in Old Testament prophecies...**

In the Old Testament the prophet, Daniel asked the meaning of the prophecy given to him, and he was told to seal it up until the time of the end.

*"And I heard, but I understood not: then said I, O my Lord, what shall be the end of these things? And he said, Go thy way, Daniel: for the words are closed up and sealed till the time of the end." (Daniel 12:8-9)*

Jesus unlocked the seal of this prophecy of Daniel in Matthew 24:15. (Incidentally we learn in Revelation 5 that He is the only One worthy to unlock any of the seals.) He said this about the Daniel prophecy:

*"When ye therefore shall see the abomination of desolation, spoken of by Daniel the prophet, stand in the holy place, (whoso readeth, let him understand:)*

**Hidden truths in Parables...**

When the disciples asked Jesus why He always spoke in parables, He replied that it was to conceal truth from some. These were truths that only the Holy Spirit could reveal. Some of those revelations would come only after Jesus had risen from the dead.

*"And the disciples came, and said unto him, Why speakest thou*

*unto them in parables? He answered and said unto them, Because it is given unto you to know the mysteries of the kingdom of heaven, but to them it is not given. For whosoever hath, to him shall be given, and he shall have more abundance: but whosoever hath not, from him shall be taken away even that he hath. Therefore speak I to them in parables: because they seeing see not; and hearing they hear not, neither do they understand."  Matthew 13:10-13*

**Things that are hidden from the natural man...**

In yet another verse Paul made it clear that only Spirit-filled people would be able to understand Spirit-filled truth.

*"But the natural man receiveth not the things of the Spirit of God: for they are foolishness unto him: neither can he know them, because they are spiritually discerned." 1Corinthians 2:14*

When studying the book of Revelation it is important to understand this. Yes, it contains literal accounts of things that have happened and of things that will happen. However, those things are all viewed from a different vantage point than what we have. The book, written by God the Father, is a gift to God the Son, and can only be understood by God the Holy Spirit.

## -The Inside View of the Eternal Christ

Jesus has sent and signified this Revelation of Himself to John, a human instrument with completely human perceptions, giving us a completely Spiritual revelation with completely human understanding.

Can you step back with me and see the picture of the Lamb and the Lion from heaven's perspective? Can you see through John's eyes the Eternal Christ in His Heavenly Home? Can you see the Second Person of the Trinity, the Fullness of the Godhead, bodily as the Old Testament Saints revealed Him to us?

Revelation is not a mystical, allegorical interpretation of anything. It is simply God's perspective of Jesus Christ. The stage is set in the Eternal Throne Room. There is a timeline, but it is distinctly present tense in its structure. The book itself explores Jesus as the Alpha and Omega the beginning and the End, and as such, traces the entire history of man and the whole story of redemption with Jesus Christ as the Hero and Central figure to the entire thing.

Think about it! John 1 tells us that Jesus (The Word) was in the beginning with God, and all things were made by Him. Paul tells us in Colossians 1:16, "For by him were all things created, that are in heaven, and that are in earth, visible and invisible….." Here in this book of Revelation, we get to see the pre-human and post-earth, eternal existence of Jesus Christ, the eternal Son of God.

Jesus said (John 1:18), "No Man hath seen God at any time: the only begotten Son, which is in the bosom of the Father, he hath declared him." Every time man talked to God in the Old Testament times he was literally talking to the Son of God. This Son of God contained the "fullness of the Godhead, bodily" (Colossians 2:9). He is the One whom all creatures (both terrestrial and celestial) have always addressed. There was no other way to see the Father except through the Son.

So… the Revelation of Jesus Christ to John, who knew Him as a man, pulled back the curtains of heaven and showed Him as He always was, is, and ever shall be: THE KING OF HEAVEN.

**Chapter:** Two

**Title:** The Basic Structure

**Summary:** The book of Revelation is written both in the present tense and in a chronological sequence. Keep in mind that human chronology and Divine chronology do not necessarily always coincide.

**Study Outline:**

1.  The Present Tense structure

2.  The Chronological structure

       A. Section One  (Chapter 1)

       B. Section Two  (Chapters 2-3)

       C. Section Three (Chapters 4-19)

       D. Section Four (Chapter 20)

       E. Section Five (Chapters 21-22)

# The Basic Structure

## -Present tense structure

Revelation is chronological in the present tense. Grammatically we have three tenses in our language: Past, present, and future. Practically we only have two tenses: Past and future. Please let me illustrate this by using this book as an example: You decided to begin to read this book—that was the future. You have now made it to the second chapter. The decision to begin is now in the past. The present is a constant moving target.

We don't understand exactly how the Great "I Am" is constantly in the present. This is a matter of faith. However, the book of Revelation demonstrates this timelessness by showing the same event from several perspectives. Sometimes it will start the story at the beginning again just to show another side of the same thing. This is an important thought to consider and might help to unravel some of the confusion in the book.

## -Chronological structure

Although the book is in the present tense, you can see a simple Chronological structure with the story that also helps to frame the book. There are basically five sections or groups of events that can be seen. These sections are identified by the players in them.

***Section one:*** (Chapter 1)This section is made up of the first chapter. It is here that we find the principal players in the event. God the Father, His Son, the Angel, and John. It is in this chapter that we find the seven churches of the new testament mentioned and the seven candlesticks of the old testament. The idea is that what is to follow includes both the old nation (Israel) and the new nation (the church). By identifying the seven churches with the seven candlesticks we learn what Ephesians 2:14 means when it says: *"For he is our peace, who hath made both one, and hath broken down the middle wall of partition between us;"*

***Section two:*** (Chapters 2-3) These chapters outline the seven different churches. There are at least four different possible applications for this section.

- The Primary Interpretation—This view defends the idea that there were seven distinctly different churches in John's day with these different characteristics. This is probably accurate but does not explain the meaning of the seven churches at this point of the Revelation. It is true but not helpful in understanding the message.

- The Practical Application– Some hold that there are seven different kinds of churches with these different characteristics. This is also a good application and can bring some healthy introspection for each church. It also is a warning to us about some of the different characters that can creep into our churches.

- Personal Acceptation—In a very similar fashion personal acceptation goes beyond the congregational assessments and focuses on our personal place in the church.

- The Prophetical Revelation– also called "The Historical view" takes its cue from Revelation 1:19 which immediately precedes this chapter, *"Write the things which thou hast seen, and the things which are, and the things which shall be hereafter;"* This verse seems to indicate that what follows is the foretelling of what is to come. According to this view,  there are seven different periods of church development over the past 2000 years. Each period of development seems to overlap the one before it and the one after it, but it is marked by complete changes in how the church conducts itself.

***Section three:*** (Chapter 4-19) This section covers the book with the seven seals. It begins with the introduction to the book, continues with the opening of the book (one seal at a time), and concludes with the final result that comes with the opening of the book.

Chapter four begins with John hearing a trumpet and a voice calling him into the heavenlies. He immediately enters the throne room and begins describing what he sees. The first thing he notices is a throne. Then he sees the One on the throne. His eyes begin taking in all of the scenes, and he describes the four and twenty elders and the sea of glass. He talks about the beasts that are "round about the throne," and describes them and their testimony. In chapter five a book is introduced with seven seals and this book seems to be a problem to everyone. No one can open it and emotion floods John as he realizes the helplessness of the situation. It is then that the Lamb, the Lion of the tribe of Judah steps forward to unseal the seven seals.

Chapters four and five set up the scene which continues until chapter nineteen. John appears to remain in the same proximate position viewing the throne and its surroundings throughout this entire section of the narrative. In chapter nineteen verses one through seven he is still in the company of the four beasts and the four and twenty elders.

As each seal is opened, it seems that the Lamb, our Advocate, is telling a story. The first six seals are almost a history lesson much like the first six chapters of Genesis where much is described in a quick overview. In chapter eight a change happens. There is silence in heaven for about half an hour. All attention seems to turn towards the earth as the horrible part of the tribulation begins to unfold. The seventh seal seems to encompass the tribulation and describe it from four different angles, much the same way that the four gospels show the earthly life of Christ.

When we get to chapter nineteen there is great rejoicing in heaven as a result of the story that has unfolded from the book with seven seals. The Bride is now allowed to wear the white robes of righteousness which are described as her wedding garment. The Bridegroom mounts up with His armies and returns to earth with the crowns of dominion on His head.

***Section four:*** (Chapter 19:11-20:15) This section briefly covers the triumphant return of Christ to earth and His subsequent millennial reign.

First, we are introduced to the complete destruction of Satan's army. Satan is seized and imprisoned in the bottomless pit for one thousand years.

The reign of Christ on earth for a thousand years (the millennium) begins with the assistance of His faithful followers. This kingdom is alluded to in Matthew 25.

At the end of The Millennium, Satan is brought up from the pit to be judged and is subsequently cast into the eternal lake of fire. The Great White Throne Judgement proceeds to bring all of the dead to be judged and they are ultimately cast into the lake of fire along with the Devil and his angels. All of the lost, who have been removed from the book of life due to their decision to reject Christ, will be cast into the lake of fire for eternity.

***Section five:*** (Chapter 21-22) This describes the marriage of the Lamb to His Bride, and the eternal life he will live with them.

In verse two of chapter twenty-one, we find the New Jerusalem prepared as a Bride adorned for her husband. Just a few verses later in verse nine she is described as "The bride, the Lambs wife." It appears that the marriage happens between these two verses. Indeed, there are many elements of a marriage ceremony described. More on this in a later chapter.

The New Jerusalem is described as the "Home Base" of the saints for all of eternity. It is not the new world but is a city that sits on the new earth. Its gates are always open, and it has no night. The Lamb is the light of the city, and He makes His home there with us.

**Chapter:** Three

**Title:** Introductions

**Summary:** Chapter one of Revelation introduces all of the main characters of the book. The entire book crystalizes around these characters.

**Study Outline:**

1. The Eternal Christ

2. The Apostle John

3. The Special Angel

4. The Believers of all time

5. The Seven churches

6. The Seven Spirits

7. The Seven Stars

# 3

# Introductions

There are some interesting things of note in the introductory chapter. It is important to stop and consider them.

## -The Eternal Christ

- Verse 1 says this is the <u>Revelation</u> of Jesus Christ

- Verse 2 says this is the <u>testimony</u> of Jesus Christ

- Verse 5 says that Jesus Christ is the <u>faithful witness</u>, reminding us that He is the first begotten from the dead and that He washed us from our sins in His own blood.

- Verse 5 also tells us that Jesus Christ is the <u>prince of the kings of the earth</u>.

- Verse 6 says that Jesus Christ <u>has made us kings and priests unto God.</u>

- Verse 8 explains to us that <u>we are in the kingdom and patience of Jesus Christ</u> along with John who is our brother.

All of these comments serve to state pointedly that Jesus Christ is central to the whole story of both this book and this life.

One of the most striking truths that comes to light in this chapter is the past, present, and future of our Lord. It is His oneness with the Almighty that becomes so apparent. Let me illustrate by quoting the references  consecutively:

- *"... him which is, and which was, and which is to come..." (vs. 4)*

- *"...which are before his throne..." (vs. 4)*

- *"...to him be glory and dominion for ever and ever..." (vs. 6)*

- *"I am Alpha and Omega, the beginning and ending, saith the Lord, which is, and which was, and which is to come, the Almighty." (vs8)*

- *" I am Alpha and Omega, the first and the last..." (vs. 11)*

- *"...one like unto the Son of man...." (vs. 13)*

- *"...Fear not: I am the first and the last." (vs. 17)*

- *"I am he that liveth, and was dead; and, behold, I am alive for evermore, Amen; and have the keys of hell and of death." (vs. 18)*

In a book where space is a premium a repetitive truth like this is imperative to notice. Jesus told the disciples in Matthew 16 that the truth of His Deity was the rock on which He would build His Kingdom. Keep this in mind as you read this passage from the book of Colossians:

*" Who is the image of the invisible God, the firstborn of every creature: For by him were all things created that are in heaven, and that are in earth, visible and invisible, whether they be thrones, or dominions, or principalities, or powers: all things were created by him, and for him: And he is before all things, and by him all things consist. And he is the head of the body, the church: who is the beginning, the firstborn from the dead; that in all things he might have the preeminence. For it pleased the Father that in him should all fulness dwell." Colossians 1:15-19 " For in him dwelleth all the fulness of the Godhead bodily." Colossians 2:9*

I believe, that the most important truth in the book of Revelation is that Jesus Christ is God. Indeed, this is the central theme of the whole Bible.

It is hard for us to wrap our heads around the Eternal Godhead. What exactly is the Trinity? We know that there is only One God. How does this work with A Father, A Son, and A Holy Spirit?

God the Father is the Source of all things. Everything proceeds from Him. All power, all beauty, all wisdom, all color, all music, absolutely all things come from Him. Because He is the Source of all, there is no way He can be contained in anything because everything comes from Him. The Bible tells us many times that God is not like us in any way. Look at these verses in this context:

*"But who is able to build him an house, seeing the heaven and heaven of heavens cannot contain him? who am I then, that I should build him an house, save only to burn sacrifice before him?" II Chronicles 2:6*

*"But will God in very deed dwell with men on the earth? behold, heaven and the heaven of heavens cannot contain thee; how much less this house which I have built!" II Chronicles 6:18*

*"These things hast thou done, and I kept silence; thou thoughtest that I was altogether such an one as thyself: but I will reprove thee, and set them in order before thine eyes." Psalm 50:21*

These verses give us a peek at the Father but never a clear image of Him. Jesus told us "No man hath seen God at any time; the only begotten Son, which is in the bosom of the Father, he hath declared him." (John 1:18) Then in John 5:37, He said, *"And the Father himself, which hath sent me, hath borne witness of me. Ye have neither heard his voice at any time, nor seen his shape."* In John 14:9 *"Jesus saith unto him, Have I been so long time with you, and yet hast thou not known me, Philip? he that hath seen me hath seen the Father; and how sayest thou then, Shew us the Father?"* In each one of these verses, Jesus seems to be trying to get us to understand that He and the Father are one (John 10:30).

This leads me to believe that every time God visited man in the Old Testament He came in the form of the Son. This Second Person of the Trinity has always been the way God has represented Himself.  The Son is the One Who walked in the garden of Eden. It was the Son in the plains of Mamre with Abram, and it was the Son in the fiery furnace of Babylon.

We see Him on His throne in Isaiah 6.  We see Him in Revelation 5 as the One on the throne in the middle of the sea of glass. There He is represented as the Lamb and the Lion of the tribe of Judah. Ezekiel describes the sea of glass as a firmament of crystal. He spends time in his first chapter describing what is under the throne,  and then in verse 26 he begins describing One that has "the likeness as the appearance of a man."  In each one of these cases, we are given a glimpse of the Eternal Son before He came as a babe to the race of man.  This is the One who is revealed in the book of Revelation. This One, Who is alive, and was dead and is "alive for evermore."

## -The Apostle John

In John 21:15-24 Jesus had a discussion with Peter about his commission. At the end of the conversation, Peter asks Jesus what John's responsibility was going to be and Jesus had this response: "If I will that he tarry till I come, what is that to thee? Follow thou me." John was quick to explain that Jesus didn't say he wasn't going to die but that if it was the Lord's will for him to still be alive at the Lord's return that it definitely was not Peter's business.

It is interesting to note that John was the only disciple who did not die a martyr's death. There are many legends and interesting stories of the miracles John performed. He was said to have raised several from the dead. According to some, he drank poison without dying. At one point the proconsul of Ephesus had him boiled alive in a cauldron of oil. After Nero's death somewhere around 81-96 A.D. during the reign of Domitian, John was exiled to Patmos where he was shown the heavenly vision we have come to know as "Revelation." After the death of Emperor Domitian, the Apostle was released and returned to Asia where it is believed that he settled at the church of Ephesus and there wrote the Gospel of John. He remained there until his death during the reign of Emperor Trajan (98-117 A.D.) according to Irenaeus (120-202 A.D.). Irenaeus claimed to have seen and heard Polycarp, a personal disciple of John and seems to be a reliable source.

It is no doubt the Revelation of the Eternal Christ on the isle of Patmos influenced the emphasis of his Epistle and set the stage for him to explain the deity of the man Jesus in his Gospel.

## -The Special Angel

There are seventy-six references to angels in the book of Revelation. John has many conversations and interactions with them. However, there appears to be this one particular angel who is his guide. We only hear from him five times.

He is referred to as the personal angel of Jesus Christ.

> *Revelation 1:1  "...sent and signified it by his angel.."*
>
> *Revelation 22:6  "...sent his angel..."*
>
> *Revelation 22:16  "...I Jesus have sent mine angel..."*

I am not sure what this means, but it is an interesting statement. Some have suggested that this could be a "Christophany," which simply means Christ in another form. I don't believe that is true for two reasons. The first reason is that Jesus Christ is now in a permanent Glorified human body. The Bible explains that God gave His only begotten Son to the human race as an eternal and everlasting gift. While Jesus appeared in the Old Testament in many forms (ie. an angel, a pillar of fire, a man, a burning bush, etc.), in the New Testament He has appeared as a man.  In Hebrews 1:6 the apostle makes it clear that Jesus is not an angel: *"And again, when he bringeth in the firstbegotten into the world, he saith, And let all the angels of God worship him."* The second reason I don't believe this angel is Jesus is that twice John tried to worship Him and was told to worship God instead.

> *Revelation 19:10  "And I fell at his feet to worship him. And he said unto me, See thou do it not: I am thy fellows-ervant, and of thy brethren that have the testimony of Jesus: worship God...."*

> *Revelation 22:8-9  " And I John saw these things, and heard them. And when I had heard and seen, I fell down to worship before the feet of the angel which shewed me these things. Then saith he unto me, See thou do it not: for I am thy fellowservant, and of thy brethren the prophets and of them which keep the sayings of this book: worship God."*

Contrast those verses with Revelation 1:17-18, which says this:

> *"And when I saw him, I fell at his feet as dead. And he laid his right hand upon me, saying unto me, Fear not; I am the first and the last: I am he that liveth, and was dead; and, behold, I am alive for evermore, Amen, and have the keys of hell and of death."*

When John fell down at the feet of Jesus to worship, he was not corrected or told to stop worshipping. Instead, Jesus introduced Himself as the Eternal God. I can only conclude then, that this angel is a special angel who was sent specifically to guide John through this amazing prophecy.

These conversations also serve as a reminder of the caution the Apostle Paul gives us in his letter to the Colossian church:

> *Colossians 2:18  "Let no man beguile you of your reward in a voluntary humility and worshipping of angels, intruding into those things which he hath not seen, vainly puffed up by his fleshly mind,"*

Many who are fascinated by the names of angels and their role in serving and protecting. Indeed, they have many interactions with mankind. Over 800 verses in the Bible deal with those interactions with us. However, our understanding of them and how they function is still very limited. Only a very few names of the angels are given in the scriptures. Some of those names like Michael, Gabriel, and Abaddon seem to have some leadership role in heaven. Some, like Lucifer and Legion, are fallen and are engaged in an anti-God activity. Because the Bible has much to say about them, a study of the angels is appropriate, but this special angel who seems to be so close to Jesus comes to us without a name and very clearly warns us not to worship him.

## -The Believers of All Time

In the first verse we are introduced to "his servants," and this seems to be a reference to the ones to whom the book is written. It is not a leap to think that the book is addressed to all who come after John, and therefore we might be quick to assume that the New Testament Church is the one being addressed.

However….,

If you let the book interpret itself, something else becomes apparent. The servants of God are all of those who have ever believed on the Lord. And here is where it gets interesting.

**Moses is called a servant**  - Rev. 15:3

**The prophets are called servants**  - Rev. 10:7, 11:18

**The church of Thyatira is called servants**  - Rev. 2:20

**Angels are called servants** - Rev. 19:10, 22:9

As we progress through the book of Revelation we find the picture of the throne room and the people present. Remember that all of these are in this one place and they are seeing the same thing that John is seeing. They are all getting the story explained at the same time.

- The One on the throne 4:1

- The 24 elders  4:4

- The Beasts on the throne  4:8

- The Lamb/ Lion on the throne  5:5-6

- The redeemed out of every kindred tongue, people and nation made to be kings and priests (refer to Rev. 1:6)  5:8-10

- The angels  5:11-12

- Every creature in heaven, on earth, under the earth, and in the sea  5:13   (refer to Romans 8:22-23)

While it is true that this event is yet to come, it is also true that it is taking place in God's throne room, a place outside of our time constraints. Therefore it is possible that anyone from any time period could be present for the Revelation of the Lamb. My conclusion is that "the servants" who are being shown this incredible Revelation of Jesus Christ include all of the believers from the Garden of Eden until the very end of time. In fact, at different times throughout the book, this incredibly large number of believers including the angels burst into a spontaneous celebration of the Lamb. If this conclusion is correct it will find support in other places in scripture. So let's see if it holds up.

**Take a look at Moses the servant.** Is it possible that he was present at this Great Redemption Explanation? Here is a man who seems to have an up close and personal look at what God is doing. The stories in the Old Testament reveal a man who saw the Glorified Son of God on the mountain and received the commandments from Him. In Matthew 5:17-19 Jesus makes it clear that He had not come to abolish the law of Moses, but to fulfill it. Which would indicate that Moses had a huge part in the Kingdom which was to come. On the mount of transfiguration (Matthew 17), we find both Moses and Elijah speaking to the Glorified Christ. Mark in chapter nine of his gospel record implies that this meeting had something to do with the kingdom of God coming with power. Peter later recounts in his second epistle that he and his friends had been "eyewitnesses" of the "majesty" of Christ. And then there is the reference in the book of Acts (Acts 7:38) of the church in the wilderness. This is a literal reference to the "called out" ones. They were considered to be part of the Kingdom of Christ.

When Jesus told Peter (Matthew 16:15-18) that He was going to build his church (otherwise known as the called out kingdom) on the truth that He was the Christ, the Son of the Living God, He was speaking of a larger group than our local independent churches. Peter refers to it in his epistle (I Peter 2:6-10) and tells us that this Cornerstone is laid in Sion (Zion), the capital city of the nation of Israel. Was Moses the servant excluded from this unveiling of the Lion of the Tribe of Judah because he lived before Pentecost? Romans eleven reminds us that we (Gentile believers) are grafted into the vine. The original branches of the vine are the people of Israel.

**Think about those things while we consider the Prophets.** James five tells us of the faith of the prophets. Peter tells us that the prophets enquired and searched diligently to find the truth of salvation (I Peter 1:10). Hebrews 11:40 says that they were not made  perfect without us. Ephesians 2:14-16 tells us that Jesus broke down the middle wall of partition between us and made both believing Israel and the believing Gentiles into one body. Romans four reminds us that Abraham was righteous because he believed God, and Paul uses that truth to explain to us how we can get saved by faith. Galatians four explains to us that we are spiritual children of Abraham. And here is another interesting find ....I Peter 3:18-20 tells us what Jesus was doing in the heart of the earth between the crucifixion and the resurrection. He was preaching in Paradise (see Luke 23:43) about what........? Those who perished in the flood are specifically mentioned. Was He explaining the Gospel to them before He took them to heaven with Him (Eph. 4:8-9)?

And then there is the verse in Ephesians (4:11) which says that

He gave the prophets to some of us for the edifying of the Body. Of course, this could refer to the prophets in the early church. However, Paul is very clear that "All Scripture" has been given to us for our edification, which would indicate that the writings of the prophets are for our learning. The prophets also have a part in the building of the body. Are they present at this great gathering of the saints?  Consider Hebrews 12:22-23,

> "But ye are come unto mount Sion, and unto the city of the living God, and heavenly Jerusalem, and to an innumerable company of angels, To the general assembly and church of the firstborn, which are written in heaven, and to God the Judge of all, and to the spirits of just men made perfect,"

**And then there is the church after Pentecost...**

The church of the age of Grace will also be present at this great event. In Revelation 4:1-2 we see a trial run of the trumpet call. This is what has been called the Rapture of the Church. It is mentioned several times in the scriptures, and at this point, John's translation into the heavens appears to be a sample of what we will expect. His account is representative of what we will see and experience when we are taken at the last trump. We will say more on this later. Take a look at the comparison verses on these topics.

- ***Voice as a Trumpet*** (4:1) In each of these verses we see a prediction of a point in time when the trumpet is going to sound a call and the redeemed will be gathered together.

  *Exodus 19:13 "There shall not an hand touch it, but he shall surely be stoned, or shot through; whether it be beast or man, it shall not live: when the trumpet soundeth long, they shall come up to the mount."*

  *Isaiah 18:3 "All ye inhabitants of the world, and dwellers on the earth, see ye, when he lifteth up an ensign on the mountains; and when he bloweth a trumpet, hear ye."*

  *Zechariah 9:14  "And the LORD shall be seen over them,*

*and his arrow shall go forth as the lightning: and the Lord GOD shall blow the trumpet, and shall go with whirlwinds of the south."*

*Matthew 24:31  "And he shall send his angels with a great sound of a trumpet, and they shall gather together his elect from the four winds, from one end of heaven to the other."*

*1Thessalonians 4:16  "For the Lord himself shall descend from heaven with a shout, with the voice of the archangel, and with the trump of God: and the dead in Christ shall rise first:"*

- **Come up hither** (4:1) In these verses we are given a peek at the call when we are told to 'Come' home.

*Song of Solomon 2:13  "The fig tree putteth forth her green figs, and the vines with the tender grape give a good smell. Arise, my love, my fair one, and come away."*

*Revelation 11:12  "And they heard a great voice from heaven saying unto them, Come up hither. And they ascended up to heaven in a cloud; and their enemies beheld them."*

*Ephesians 1:10  "That in the dispensation of the fulness of times he might gather together in one all things in Christ, both which are in heaven, and which are on earth; even in him:"*

*John 11:52  "And not for that nation only, but that also he should gather together in one the children of God that were scattered abroad."*

- **Immediately...in the spirit** (4:2) These verses have to do with the immediate change that takes place when the trumpet sounds.

*1Thessalonians 4:13-17  "But I would not have you to be ignorant, brethren, concerning them which are asleep, that ye sorrow not, even as others which have no hope. For if we be-*

*lieve that Jesus died and rose again, even so them also which sleep in Jesus will God bring with him. For this we say unto you by the word of the Lord, that we which are alive and remain unto the coming of the Lord shall not prevent them which are asleep. For the Lord himself shall descend from heaven with a shout, with the voice of the archangel, and with the trump of God: and the dead in Christ shall rise first: Then we which are alive and remain shall be caught up together with them in the clouds, to meet the Lord in the air: and so shall we ever be with the Lord."*

*1Corinthians 15:52 "In a moment, in the twinkling of an eye, at the last trump: for the trumpet shall sound, and the dead shall be raised incorruptible, and we shall be changed."*

All of these verses seem to indicate that the church will be gathered together when the trumpet sounds, and immediately translated into the heavens like Enoch and Elijah.

**And don't forget the angels....**

According to I Peter 1:12 even the angels are interested in the Gospel story. It is easy to overlook the fact that the whole creation is struggling because of sin. Lucifer was the first to fall and Revelation twelve indicates that one-third of all the angels went with him. Daniel 10:12-13 reveals that sometimes the messages that are to be delivered by the angels get waylaid. Gabriel explained to Daniel that Michael, "One of the chief princes," had to come and help him get free from the prince of Persia, who was hindering him from coming to Daniel. For eons of time, it appears that this struggle has been waged in the heavens. Ephesians six explains to us that we also have been engaged in this struggle against the "principalities and powers in heavenly places." In Revelation 12:7-11 we are told that Michael and his angels finally defeat the dragon. The interesting thing is that this war finally comes to a close and the Dragon is cast out of heaven, not because of the efforts of the angels, but instead by the blood of the

Lamb and the testimony of the brethren.

**The twenty-four elders** are a curious lot. They are referenced twelve times in Revelation. It is not until we get to the New Jerusalem in Revelation twenty-one that we begin to get a clue about who they might be. The New Jerusalem is built upon the twelve apostles and on the gates are the names of the twelve tribes. As we progress through the book of Revelation it appears that two groups of people are represented as saints. Revelation seven has the clearest presentation. There is 144,000 called from the twelve tribes, and then there is the group which no man can number from all tribes and nations. Chapter eleven also refers to these two groups. Revelation 12:17 calls them the remnant of the seed of the woman; "which keep the commandments of God, and have the testimony of Jesus Christ." Two groups of believers: Old Testament saints, and New Testament saints are both represented by the twenty-four elders.

Another fascinating scriptural parallel is found in the Levitical leadership established by King David in I Chronicles 24:4. Of the Four sons of Aaron only two lived to continue in the priesthood, Eleazar and Ithamar. Of these two families, David appointed sixteen from Eleazar's family and eight from Ithamar's family to be the chiefs over the work of the Lord's house. That is a total of twenty-four Levitical Priesthood heads. Each one served in his own course which lasted for a period of two-weeks. The priests numbered in the thousands and therefore could not be all present at the same time. So whenever, these 24 elders would get together the entire priesthood would be represented by them. This is a beautiful example of the representative priesthood around the throne of David in heaven.

## -The Seven Churches

This book is specifically written to the seven churches according to the fourth verse of chapter one. One must ask the question: Why are these seven specific churches chosen and not any of the larger congregations in other places? Why were the churches in Asia addressed in this eternal Revelation of Christ and not the churches of Egypt, Israel, or Europe? The most likely answer is that these seven churches seem to parallel every phase of the church for the past 20 centuries.

It is interesting to note that they are described in Rev. 1:20 as the golden candlesticks which were so prominent in the tabernacle of the wilderness and the only light source of that tabernacle. Some have suggested that the seven feasts of Leviticus 23 and the kingdom parables of Matthew parallel these seven distinctly different stages of the Age of Grace.

The names of the churches also seem to bear some significance.

Ephesus = Desirable

Smyrna = myrrh

Pergamos = "though married"

Thyatira = incense

Sardis = remnant

Philadelphia = brotherly love

Laodicea = voice of the people

A study of the history of the church will show these comparisons which seem to go well beyond mere coincidence. We will discuss this further in another chapter.

## -The Seven Spirits

In this introduction of Revelation, we are also introduced to the seven Spirits of God which are before His throne (Rev. 1:4). It is not the last time we read of them. So who are these seven Spirits? If you believe in the Trinity, as I do, this idea of the seven Spirits of God is a little bit disconcerting. It doesn't quite seem to fit into our theological structure at least not simply. So what do we do with it?

When you are learning about God, you are better off not trying to fit Him into your ideas. Instead, you should just learn what He says about Himself, and take Him as He is. So let's do that with this discovery.

Ephesians 4:4 is clear that there is only one Holy Spirit, "There is one body, and one Spirit, even as ye are called in one hope of your calling;" In Genesis 1:2 we are introduced to the Spirit of God for the first time. The scriptures clearly indicate that there is only One Who is the third person of the Trinity. These seven spirits, therefore can not possibly be referring to part of the Godhead.

They are mentioned four times specifically. Each one of these verses tells us something significant about these seven Spirits.

> #1 *"John to the seven churches which are in Asia: Grace be unto you, and peace, from him which is, and which was, and which is to come; and from **the seven Spirits which are before his throne**;" Rev. 1:4*

The first thing we learn about the Seven Spirits in this verse is that the letter to the seven churches is as much from the Seven Spirits as it is from Christ, Himself. It very clearly says that the message is from "Him.....and from the seven Spirits." So, at the very least, they are closely connected to the heart and mind of God. They are most definitely involved in the delivery of the message.

> #2 *"And unto the angel of the church in Sardis write; These things saith he that hath **the seven Spirits of God**, and the seven stars; I know thy works, that thou hast a name that thou livest, and art dead." Rev.3:1*

From this verse, we learn that God looks upon them as something He has. Interestingly, He puts them together with the seven stars which He later says are the angels of the seven churches. Once again we can deduce that they are part of giving the message. The letter was from them and now we find out that they are part of the vehicle by which the message is broadcast.

*#3 "And out of the throne proceeded lightnings and thunderings and voices: and there were seven lamps of fire burning before the throne, which are **the seven Spirits of God**." Rev. 4:5*

In this verse, we find them as part of the scenery around the throne. They are represented as lamps. In Hebrews 9:23-24 we read:

*"It was therefore necessary that the patterns of things in the heavens should be purified with these; but the heavenly things themselves with better sacrifices than these. For Christ is not entered into the holy places made with hands, which are the figures of the true; but into heaven itself, no to appear in the presence of God for us:"*

The apostle is suggesting here and in other verses that the furniture of the tabernacle was simply patterns or shadows of the things in heaven. When we go back to the original construction of the wilderness tabernacle we find these words in Exodus 25:40:

*"And look that thou make them after their pattern, which was shewed thee in the mount." It appears that the candlestick and the ark of the covenant are only imitations of the things in heaven.*

This causes me to stop and go take another look at Revelation 1:12-13:

*"And I turned to see the voice that spake with me. And being turned, I saw seven golden candlesticks: and in the midst of the seven candlesticks one like unto the Son of man, clothed with a garment down to the foot, and girt about the paps with a golden girdle."*

Is it possible that the view John had on Patmos of the Son of man in the midst of the candlesticks is the same as his view of the Lamb in the midst of the throne surrounded by the seven lamps? It appears to be the same scene. The first scene is viewed on earth. The second scene is viewed in heaven.

The seven candlesticks of Revelation 1:20 are identified as the seven churches. The seven lamps must be the Spirit of God manifested in those seven churches.

> #4 *"And I beheld, and, lo, in the midst of the throne and of the four beasts, and in the midst of the elders, stood a Lamb as it had been slain, having seven horns and seven eyes, **which are the seven Spirits of God** sent forth into all the earth.' Rev. 5:6*

In this verse, we find out that these are seven specific spirits sent forth unto all the earth. These are not the only spirits that have been sent from the throne to the earth. Zechariah 6:1-5 mentions four chariots that are sent out into the earth from the throne room. Each chariot is led by different colored horses that look suspiciously similar to the four different colored horses of the first four seals in Revelation 6. Verse 5 says:

> *"And the angel answered and said unto me, These are the four spirits of the heavens, which go forth from standing before the Lord of all the earth."*

These are not the same spirits as the seven.

In I Samuel 16:14 the Bible surprises us with the truth that Saul was troubled by an evil spirit that came from the Lord. Then in I Kings 22:20-23, we are given a backstage look at a discussion in the heavens in which the Lord is looking for a way to cause Ahab to get himself in a corner. A lying spirit comes before the Lord and says that it will convince Ahab to put himself in the compromising position required for the Lord's will to be done. God sends the lying spirit and Ahab listens and is consequently killed.

I put these references here to illustrate that there are multiple spirits at the disposal of our Lord. David reminds us in his Psalm that God has many ministers who could be called spirits or even Angels.

> *"Who maketh his angels spirits; his ministers a flaming fire."* *Psalms 104:4*

If we keep these references in their context we are drawn to the parallels with the candlestick in Revelation 1:20. And then to the first church and its candlestick (Revelation 2:5) being removed. Immediately, our minds go to what the candlestick represents in the teachings of Christ while He was on this earth:

> *Matthew 5:14-16 "Ye are the light of the world, A city that is set on an hill cannot be hid. Neither do men light a candle, and put it under a bushel, but on a candlestick and it giveth light unto all that are in the house. Let your light so shine before men, that they may see your good works, and glorify your Gather which is in heaven."*

> *Matthew 6:22-23 "The light of the body is the eye: if therefore thine eye be single, thy whole body shall be full of light. But if thine eye be evil, thy whole body shall be full of darkness. If therefore the light that is in thee be darkness, how great is that darkness!"*

> *Ephesians 5:8 "For ye were sometimes darkness, but now are ye light in the Lord: walk as children of light:"*

> *1John 1:7 "But if we walk in the light, as he is in the light, we have fellowship one with another, and the blood of Jesus Christ his Son cleanseth us from all sin."*

Each of these verses indicates that light is very much a part of our testimony and our identity as believers and as a part of the body of Christ.

Is it possible that these seven spirits are actually seven different ways that God has dealt with man throughout the age of Grace? Is it possible that these seven spirits represent the light that is given to the world through these different churches? It seems so to me. It is interesting to note that there are seven distinctly different covenants in the Old Testament and the seven church ages are given the benefits claimed in those old covenants. More on that later.

## -The Seven Stars

Revelation 1:20 clearly states that these seven stars in the right hand of the Lord are the angels of the seven churches. The Greek word used here is αγγελοι (angeloi) which means messenger.

There are a couple of surface ideas about whom they could represent. One idea is that they are the guardian angels of each church or church age. This idea does not seem to have support in any of the early writings of the church of which I have access. The second idea is that they might represent the pastors of the churches. If you believe that these seven churches represent seven specific local churches in Asia and nothing more, then you might subscribe to that idea quickly and move on.

In 1883 Dr. William Milligan, the professor of Divinity and Biblical Criticism in the University of Aberdeen released his commentary on the Book of Revelation. His comments were some of the best on this subject in my opinion, and so I would like to share them with you:

> "The true idea seems to be that the "angels" of the churches are a symbolical representation in which the active, as distinguished from the passive, life of the Church finds expression. To St. John every person, every thing, has its angel. God proclaims and executes His will by angels. He addresses even the Son by an angel. The Son acts and reveals His truth by an angel. The waters have an angel. Fire has an angel. The winds have an angel. The abyss has an angel. On all these occasions the "angel" is interposed when the persons or things spoken of are represented as coming out of themselves and as taking their part in intercourse or in action. In like manner the "angels of the churches" are the churches themselves, with this mark of distinction only, that, when they are thus spoken of, they are viewed not merely as in possession of inward vigour, but as exercising it towards things without."

It is fascinating that these angels are represented as stars. Again we see a parallel between light and the testimony of the church in a universal way. They are not here represented as a candlestick but as stars in the heavens. Indicating that the Church of Jesus Christ is Universal in its ministry. Ephesians points this out: "To the intent that now unto the principalities and powers in heavenly places might be known by the church the manifold wisdom of God, According to the eternal purpose which he purposed in Christ Jesus our Lord:" (Ephesians 3:10-11). There is the earthly ministry of the Church also represented by the candlesticks. There is the heavenly ministry represented by the seven flames before the throne. But this third look describing these spirits as angels encompasses both heaven and earth, as well as, the heavenly places outside the throne room of God.

As we head in this direction in our understanding of just what an angel is, we are reminded that God represents Himself and His will in various forms. According to John 3:16 we find that God gave His only Begotten Son to the human race. This Only Begotten Son was distinguished from the Angels in the past as being the "fullness of the Godhead bodily" (Colossians 2:9). The Son is the One we see on the eternal throne. He is the One whom Lucifer has attempted to replace since before time began. The Father manifests Himself through the Son and always has done so. However, His will is carried out through the creation and subsequent obedience of a multitude of messengers who represent Him in so many different ways.

The angels of the church are the active and aggressive will of God being carried out in a spiritual and animated body. I can not even hope to completely grasp the concept in my human body, but can only try to describe what John describes through spiritual eyes. This seems to me the most honest explanation of the Seven Stars.

In Summary, these seven different characters are found throughout the book of Revelation as the main participants in the drama which unfolds in the Heaven of heavens.

# Section 2

**Chapter:** Four

**Title:** The Seven Churches

**Summary:** Chapters two and three discuss the seven different churches and their role in the drama.

**Study Outline:**

1.  Different applications of the Seven Churches
2.  The Church as the Mystery Kingdom
3.  The Historical Church Ages
4.  The Parallel Kingdom Parables
5.  The Restoration of the Old Covenant blessings

**4**

# The Seven Churches

## -Different Applications

In Chapters two and three we find letters written to seven different churches. Just what do these letters mean, and what do they have to do with us?

Over the centuries scholars have pondered their meaning and tried to draw applications from them. All of the opinions seem to boil down to about four different applications. After studying each of the opinions, I, personally, have become comfortable with the idea that all of them are correct.

**Primary Interpretation.** The primary interpretation is that there were seven different churches in Asia at the time John was exiled on Patmos. Those seven different local churches each had specific problems that needed to be addressed. In much the same way which the Lord dealt with the New Testament churches through the Apostle Paul's epistles, the Lord had things to say to those specific seven churches of Asia through the Apostle John. Some statements would have been local references that each church would understand. For example: The "lukewarm" reference to Laodicea and the subsequent "I will spue thee out" might have been a reference to the Laodicean water situation.

Some have suggested that it could be a reference to the Meander River which lazily wound its way through the Laodicean countryside resulting in a tepid water temperature. Visitors passing through being acquainted with the hot springs of Hierapolis and the cold springs of Colossi would have been completely disgusted by the foul tasting river waters of the Meander.

Herodotus spoke of an aqueduct that brought water to Laodicea. Because of the ingenuity of the aqueduct, the Laodiceans were quite proud of it. However, due to the six miles the water traveled, the temperature would have been lukewarm at best. Because it did not pass through any purification the water would have become unclean and undrinkable making anyone sick who tried to drink it.

Still another story mentions a well in Laodicea which was lukewarm in the morning, reached its coldest at noon, and was boiling hot at midnight. Any of these references would have been understandable to the Laodicean people, and, therefore, would have explained to them their spiritual state.

These stories bring value to the idea that the letters to the churches had a practical purpose in helping the specific churches of Asia.

**Practical Application.** At the time of this writing, there are an estimated 37 million Christian churches worldwide, and approximately 34,000 different denominations. No matter how hard we try to clone ourselves, no two churches are exactly alike. The differences can be seen in how we interpret the Bible, how we worship, what our community looks like, who we learn from, etc. Not all Christian churches operate with the power of God and some could be considered imposters and apostates. However, your local assembly is not the only Body of Christ, and, therefore, you must assume that different assembly practices are not necessarily incorrect. It is with this thought in mind that we consider the possibility there may be seven different kinds of churches that represent Christ.

Your church may be like the church of Ephesus which is correct doctrinally. The lesson to learn is that doctrinal soundness can lead to a lack of love and grace.

Your church might be like Sardis, struggling to stay alive. The Lord encourages you to "Be watchful, and strengthen the things which remain, that are ready to die." Don't give up. The power of God can still breathe life into the glowing embers that remain.

Maybe your church is like Philadelphia which has no end of open ministry doors. The caution to Philadelphia is that the synagogue of Satan is also in the vicinity and must be guarded against.

Possibly, your church is like Laodicea, "rich and increased with goods and have need of nothing." To you, the challenge is the slippery slide into lukewarmness, and you are encouraged to overcome anyway.

As you can see there are multiple lessons to be learned by evaluating the type of church you are in. If you are a pastor or church leader and are trying to figure out what is wrong with your particular assembly, I would encourage you to assess yourselves with these seven different models and discover the keys to a successful church right there in the text.

**Personal Acceptation.** In a very similar fashion personal acceptation goes beyond the congregational assessments and focuses on our personal place in the church. Listed here are the actions of the different kinds of people we find in the churches:

- Labouring and not fainting
- Patient
- Judging righteously
- Legalistically dominating other believers (Nicolaitans)
- Enduring tribulation
- Lying about being Jews
- Staying faithful unto death
- Allowing Satan a seat in the church

- Holding fast the Name of Christ
- Holding the doctrine of Balaam (Spiritual fornication)
- Being charitable
- Maintaining Faith
- Allowing Jezebel to teach and seduce inside the church
- Knowing the depths of Satan and being participants
- Being weak
- Having a reputation for life when there is no life
- Keeping Spiritual garments undefiled
- Having a little strength
- Keeping the Word
- Not denying the Name of Jesus
- Maintaining lukewarm works
- Being spiritually wretched, miserable, poor, blind and naked
- Being willing to repent
- Overcoming the World, the Flesh, and the Devil

In the Church, then, there seems to be a variety of types of individuals. Some are victorious overcomers, and some are weak and barely showing the light they profess.

Still others in the church appear to have given a place to Satan. This fact should cause us to pause when we consider the time when Jesus called Peter out for doing the work of Satan (Matthew 16:23). Judas allowed Satan to enter into him. Ananias and Saphira allowed Satan to fill their heart with lies. There is also a mention in Acts 13:35 of devout people being stirred up by the Jews to be used of Satan to persecute the church. In Ephesians 5:26 Paul warns us not to give the devil a place in our lives. The local church is full of all kinds of people some are saved and some are tools of Satan.

There are also faithful people in the church who are pleasing to the Lord and are full of good works. Those are the kinds of people that we should be.

**Prophetic Revelation.** This classical view of the seven church ages draws a parallel between each church and a corresponding time in history. Many commentators and Bible historians in the last couple hundred years have discovered striking parallels between different periods of church history and the descriptions of these churches.

As we mentioned in an earlier chapter, Revelation is a chronological story, and so, if we begin with John's place in history and look forward to our time, we can see several seismic shifts in how the church does its business.

We are watching such a shift happen before our eyes at this moment. Churches have been engaged in worldwide mission work. We have attempted great things for God and have seen lives and cultures completely changed by the message of the Gospel. However, gradually, we have seen the church begin to look wealthy. Pastors are paid large sums of money and churches are equipped with all of the latest sound and video equipment. Marketing teams are employed to capture the attention of people. Our messages have gotten more cosmopolitan so as not to offend anyone who has a different opinion. Little by little the church platform has begun to look like a concert event, and the pulpit is being moved out of sight. Things that were considered sins are now looked on as sicknesses and are coddled rather than condemned. People can be what they wish through the week with no thought of condemnation from the church body. Slowly but surely we have become less effective in changing lives and behaviors and have taken on the look of Laodicea.

It is not difficult to defend this position when looking through the historical documents of the church. I believe it is a viable explanation and should be given some attention. We will deal with this more later.

## -The Church as the Mystery Kingdom

Before we explore the historical church ages we need to step back and discuss what the church really is. The word, "church" is translated from the Greek word "εκκλησια." This word simply means called out and is a reference to those who have been called out of darkness into the light of Christ. I Peter 2:9 puts it this way:

> *"But ye are a chosen generation, a royal priesthood, an holy nation, a peculiar people; that ye should shew forth the praises of him who hath **called you out** of darkness into his marvellous light:"*

The word "Church" itself has an interesting if somewhat elusive etymology. There are differing opinions on why it was used as the translation of εκκλησια (ekklesia). Tyndale's 1525 translation used the word "Congregacion" to translate the word in Matthew 16:18. The Great Bible of 1539, and the Bishops Bible of 1568 also followed suit. Enzinas in his Spanish Bible 1543 did a transliteration of the word and landed on *Yglelia* as the proper expression. The Spanish Scio Bible of 1793 changed it to *iglesia* and all of the Spanish Bibles since have used that word.

Why did the King James translators not follow the Bishops Bible, which was their core document, nor the Tyndale translation, which they followed over 80% of the time? The simple reason is that King James, when he commissioned the translators to put together his authorized text, outlined 15 rules which he expected them to follow. Rule #3 states this: "The Old Ecclesiastical Words to be kept, viz. the Word Church not to be translated Congregation &c." Specifically, this word was addressed by the King. He wanted the word "church" to be used so as to maintain the old ecclesiastical terms. Whether or not King James actually produced these rules or, if it was in fact his Bishop, Richard Bancroft, who determined this, I don't know.

Some have suggested that the word finds its roots in the Old English word *circe* from which we get our words circle and circus. The hypothesis is that the original congregants met in a circle and therefore the assembly became known as "the circle." Others have attached a pagan significance to the circle. Stating that all of the pagans would assemble in circles and call them by that name and therefore this word was used so they would understand the concept of the assembly. Other language sources would include the Old Saxon *kirika*, Old Norse *kirja*, Dutch *kerk*, German *kirche*.

It is also interesting to note that the Greek word *kyriakon* which means "of the Lord" was used to refer to houses of Christian worship since 300 A.D., especially in the east. It was picked up by the Slavic tongues possibly through direct Greek-to-Germanic transmission. From the Old Church Slavonic language, we have the word *criky*, in Russian *cerkov*, in Finnish *kirkko*,  and Estonian *kirrik*.

A combination of these reasons might have caused the word *church* to become the translation for εκκλησια. So, when people would gather together they would be going to "the circle" (ie. Kirche) or the assembly "of the Lord" (ie. kirrkko) and so gradually they would begin defining it with those words. After the Reformation, the anglicized form of those words, *"church"* became used almost exclusively to describe an assembly of believers regardless of denomination.

In Summary, William Tyndale used a dynamic equivalent of *ekklesia* when he used the word *congregacion*. His choice of words would have hermeneutically identified the congregation of the children of Israel as the *ekklesia*. This would only be partly correct as we understand that the Gentiles also have a part in the church, but it obviously fell short of the meaning. The King James translators also used a dynamic equivalent when they used *church* as the translation of this word. Their choice helped the English-speaking world to understand that this was a new thing. It wasn't just the nation of Israel being spoken of here, but indeed the circle of worship which was being recognized worldwide as the followers of Christ– this new "assembly of the Lord" - was indeed something more than the congregation of Israel. The body of Christ has accepted this word and attempted to continually define it.

The reason we have devoted this space to this discussion is to highlight the fact that sometimes a translation of a word or a dynamic equivalent of a word does not completely capture the full meaning of the word in its original language, and in this specific case there is more to the story. We don't need to change the word. We just need to understand it.

Which leads us to the question: What did Jesus mean when He said, *"...Upon this rock I will build my church; and the gates of hell shall not prevail against it."* (Matthew 16:18)? Was He referencing a local independent assembly of believers? Was He referring to what some have called the "Universal Church"? Or would it be better to say that this is a Kingdom reference? Is the Kingdom of Christ and the Church the same thing?

The Old Testament often makes comments alluding to this Mystery Kingdom which is eternal. Balaam was a pagan prophet who started explaining this mystery Kingdom:

> *"He hath said, which heard the words of God, and knew the knowledge of the most High, which saw the vision of the Almighty, falling into a trance, but having his eyes open: I shall see him, but not now: I shall behold him, but not nigh: there shall come a Star out of Jacob, and a Sceptre shall rise out of Israel, and shall smite the corners of Moab, and destroy all the children of Sheth." Numbers 24:16-17*

Isaiah also prophesied of this kingdom which was to be eternal:

> *"For unto us a child is born, unto us a son is given: and the government shall be upon his shoulder: and his name shall be called Wonderful, Counsellor, The mighty God, The everlasting Father, The Prince of Peace. Of the increase of his gov-*

*ernment and peace there shall be no end, upon the throne of David, and upon his kingdom, to order it, and to establish it with judgment and with justice from henceforth even for ever. The zeal of the LORD of hosts will perform this." Is. 9:6-7*

Isaiah begins referencing it as a mountain that will be a habitation for all nations. This mountain reference is also reiterated in the book of Daniel chapter two, which most notably deals with the dream of Nebuchadnezzar:

*"And it shall come to pass in the last days, that the mountain of the LORD'S house shall be established in the top of the mountains, and shall be exalted above the hills; and all nations shall flow unto it." Isaiah 2:2*

*"Then was the iron, the clay, the brass, the silver, and the gold, broken to pieces together, and became like the chaff of the summer threshingfloors; and the wind carried them away, that no place was found for them: and the stone that smote the image became a great mountain, and filled the whole earth." Daniel 2:35*

The church then must be the kingdom prophesied of throughout the Old Testament. It is built upon the Stone "cut out without hands" from Daniel 2. The apostle Paul calls this the "mystery of Christ" in Ephesians 3. He also says that it is a mystery "...which from the beginning of the world hath been hid in God..."

Peter in his first epistle in the second chapter gives a nod to this Kingdom stating that we are a new nation built upon the Chief cornerstone, Jesus Christ. Of course, it is easy to tie this to Nebuchadnezzar's dream (Daniel 2) where we find the reference to a rock cut out without man's hands which crushes the kingdoms of the world and becomes a mountain filling the whole earth. This Rock shows up multiple times in scripture starting with Exodus 17:6.

The New Testament continues the idea of the Kingdom built on this Rock:

*"Therefore whosoever heareth these sayings of mine, and doeth them, I will liken him unto a wise man, which built his house upon a rock:" Matthew 7:24*

*"As it is written, Behold, I lay in Sion a stumblingstone and rock of offence: and whosoever believeth on him shall not be ashamed." Romans 9:33*

*"And did all drink the same spiritual drink: for they drank of that spiritual Rock that followed them: and that Rock was Christ." 1Corinthians 10:4*

*"Ye also, as lively stones, are built up a spiritual house, an holy priesthood, to offer up spiritual sacrifices, acceptable to God by Jesus Christ. Wherefore also it is contained in the scripture, Behold, I lay in Sion a chief corner stone, elect, precious: and he that believeth on him shall not be confounded. Unto you therefore which believe he is precious: but unto them which be disobedient, the stone which the builders disallowed, the same is made the head of the corner, And a stone of stumbling, and a rock of offence, even to them which stumble at the word, being disobedient: whereunto also they were appointed." 1Peter 2:5 -8*

Matthew devotes much space in his gospel to describing the mystery Kingdom of the Christ. Sometimes the New Testament defines it as the "Body of Christ" and sometimes as the "Bride" of Christ. This Mystery Kingdom is not of this world according to Jesus (John 18:36). In Revelation 17-18 it delivers a decisive blow on the mystery kingdom of the world, again referenced in Daniel 2 and named mystery Babylon in Revelation 17.

In Galatians 4 we find that it is described as the spiritual seed of Abraham. It is the complete fulfillment of every everlasting covenant in the Old Testament. It is a nation and a kingdom that is both spiritual and physical. Knowing that spiritual things, which we can not see in this world, are very real and visual from God's viewpoint, we can make sense of the overlap of spiritual and physical explanations. This understanding is critical to the under-standing of the book of Revelation as a whole.

## -The Historical Church Ages

### 1st) The Church of Ephesus  33-67A.D.

There are some differences of opinion about the exact dates for these churches and to be sure it is difficult to nail down the actual dates. The Apostle Paul founded the Ephesian church sometime around the end of the reign of Emperor Claudius, which was in the year 54 A.D. His letter to the Ephesian church was posted about 61 A.D. The book of Ephesians is full of commendations concerning their faithfulness to the truth and it encourages them to love each other as Christ loved the church. We can see glimps-es of their characteristics in Revelation 2:1-7.

Listed as the first church in Revelation it is not a stretch to con-sider that this is actually a snapshot view of the first period of the church. Many historians use the death of John (somewhere be-tween 100 and 120 AD.) as the ending of this segment of church history. It is commonly referred to as the Apostolic Church age. During this time the apostles worked to establish the foundation of the church and were subsequently martyred in the process.

My calculations based on research and Bible passages place the ending of this church age close to the same time that Jerusalem was besieged by Emperor Titus. The church at this time seemed to be losing some of it's fervor and heresies were prevalent.

Identifying characteristics:

- Works
- Labour
- Patience
- Tried fake apostles found them liars
- Hadn't fainted with the load of responsibility

- ♦ Left their first love

- ♦ Hated the deeds of the Nicolaitans

## 2nd) The Church of Smyrna  67-312 A.D.

The second church age is characterized by suffering. There are fake Jews during this time who have rejected the sacrifice of Christ. There is a specific reference to 10 days of persecution which correlates to the 10 different persecutions by 10 different Roman Emperors beginning with Nero.

Emperor Domitian exiled John to the isle of Patmos near the end of his reign. Eusebius claims that this happened in the year 97 A.D. Although Irenaeus claimed that Domitian died in 96 A.D. So there is a slight timeline discrepancy.

Irenaeus (180 A.D.) was a student of Polycarp who was a student of John the Apostle. In his writings, we find the statement that Johns vision on the isle of Patmos "was seen no very long time since, but almost in our day, towards the end of Domitian's reign." (*Against Heresies  Book V chapter XXX paragraph 3.*)

Clement of Alexandria (150-215 A.D.) says that John returned from the isle of Patmos "after the death of the Tyrant." Domitian was undoubtedly being referred to here. Although he was popular with the people, the Roman Senate despised him because he set himself up as the supreme ruler and disregarded them almost completely. Whereupon the Senate conspired to kill him and subsequently assassinated him.  Eusebius in his *Ecclesiastical History III* also seems to support the idea that Domitian was the "Tyrant" referenced in Clement's works.

In the third, fourth, and fifth centuries the church continued to teach that  John's Apocalypse was penned after the death of Domitian. Victorinus (230–303 A.D.), Jerome (340-420 A.D.) Sozomen (400-450 A.D.) all confirmed the timeline mentioned by Eusebius.

In 1684 John Fox wrote his book *The Acts and Monuments of Matters Most Special and Memorable Happening in the Church* (often called Foxe's Book of Martyrs in its abridged form). He makes the claim that following his exile John returned to Ephesus and from there continued to govern the church as the chief Apostle until the time of Emperor Trajan (98-117 A.D.). It seems that from Ephesus, then, he wrote first the Book of Revelation, followed by the Gospel of John, and his last three epistles which also bear his name. Of course, this explains why the Gospel of John spends so much time on the Deity of Christ. John was the only Apostle who witnessed the Glory of our Eternal Christ before he penned his Gospel record.

These dates and historical findings completely irradicate the theory of the preterists, who claim that the book of Revelation was fulfilled by 70 A.D. and therefore has no impact on any last-day fulfillments. The term preterism comes from the Latin praeter, meaning "past." So then, preterism is the view that the biblical prophecies concerning the "end times" have already been fulfilled—in the past. Evidently, preterism had already appeared before the completion of the New Testament Scriptures. Paul called out Hymenaeus and Philetus for teaching that the resurrection was past already and soundly rebuked them for heresy (II Timothy 2:16-19) Since Revelation was written after the death of Domitian in 96 or 97 A.D. and during the reign of Trajan in 98 to 117 A.D., it could not possibly have had any reference to the destruction of Jerusalem by Titus in 70 A.D.

Identifying characteristics:

- Works

- Tribulation

- Poverty

- Blasphemy of fake Jews

- 10 days of persecution

### 3rd) The Church of Pergamos 313-590 A.D.

The city of Pergamos was known for providing a royal residence to a long succession of kings. It had a celebrated library that boasted over 200,000 books second only to the library of Alexandria. It was in this city that the art of preparing animal skins for writing was perfected. Some have suggested that many of the extant manuscripts (MS) were prepared first in this city. It was also in this city that the famed temple of Aesculapius resided. The most prominent statue was one of a wreathed serpent who was identified as the Preserver and Saviour medicinally.

The name Pergamos is loosely translated as "married to the tower." It seems to be a reference to the church's relationship with the Mystery Babylon or the world governing system.

During this period Constantine encouraged the church to be more cosmopolitan and inclusive. After the extreme persecutions of the past emperors, it was a relief to find favor in the government. However, it turned bad when the church began to explore ways to coexist with idolatry. Balac is specifically referenced as an illustration of this issue. The pressure was not to reject the world and its idolatry but to absorb it. We find our modern celebrations of Easter and Christmas to find their root here. Many pagan practices including the prayers to the saints and the worship of statues and relics were introduced as Christian practices during this time.

Identifying characteristics:

- Works
- Satan had a seat here
- Faithful martyr
- Doctrine of Balaam
- Doctrine of Nicolaitans

## 4th) The Church of Thyatira 590-1170 A.D.

Gregory the Great, considered by many to be the founder of the medieval papacy, began his ecclesiastical career in 574 as a deacon of the Roman church. In 590 he became the pope and was considered a master organizer. According to the Encyclopedia Britannica:

> "In conducting war, he planned strategies, funded soldiers, and directed diplomacy, twice preventing Rome from being sacked by the Lombards. He also ransomed hostages, supported refugees, secured the grain supply, and repaired aqueducts."

With the use of the sword, he brought many into the fold of the Roman church and continued to aggressively blend paganism and Christianity. Jezebel is specifically referenced here because of her persecution of the truth and her effort to blend paganism and Judaism.

This was a horrible time for the church and is painted as the "depths of Satan" and a time of death. We call it "The Dark Ages."

It would be a mistake not to mention the rise of Islam during this time. The writers of the last century referred to it as the "Mohammedan" religion because of they adhered to the teachings of Mohammed. His career as a prophet and reformer began in 610 A.D. and continued until his death in 632 A.D. The blend of the Christian faith into this hybrid religion is interesting. Islam teaches that Jesus was a great prophet, that He died and rose from the grave three days later. It also teaches the return of Christ to reign in the world victoriously but fails to understand the eternity of Christ. In Mecca, there are two graves. One contains the bones of Mohammed and the other one (close by) has the inscription of the name of Jesus. It is empty, of course, but is prepared for the day when they believe He will die again a second time and be immortally enshrined in the tomb. When they pray to Mecca, it is toward these two tombs that they pray.

The Greek Orthodox church also bears some note. In 1054 A.D. the Latin Pope and the Greek Patriarch each pronounced the other church to be excommunicated. The Roman church continued to grow in power dominating the state, while the Greek church distanced itself from the affairs of the state.

While the Greek and Roman churches were fighting, the Roman church also began its crusades against the Mohammedans. The basic reason had to do with the control of Jerusalem. There were seven principal crusades which all failed to rest control from the Moslems. Due to these crusades, the power and influence of the Roman church gained much ground even though they failed to succeed in their main objective.

During this time some faithful saints tried to right the ship. Anselm was born in 1033 A.D. in Piedmont Italy and wrote many theological works. He has been called "a second Augustine," and suffered banishment for a little while. Peter Abelard (1079 to 1142 A.D.) is regarded as the founder of the University of Paris. His daring challenges to the Roman church brought crowds to hear him and also brought him under several bans from the church. Bernard of Clairvaux (1091-1153 A.D.) wrote some of the hymns we sing today. Two of the most famous hymns are: "Jesus, the Very Thought of Thee" and "O Sacred Head, now wounded."

Identifying characteristics:

- Works
- Charity
- Faith
- Patience
- Last works
- Place for Jezebel
- Spiritual adultery

- Great tribulation

- Depths of Satan

- Hold fast to what they have

## 5th) The Church of Sardis  1170-1750 A.D.

The word Sardis means "escaping ones." This seems to be referencing the escape of the protestant church from the clutches of idolatrous doctrines of the previous two church ages. The challenge to them was to "strengthen the things which remain" and "are ready to die."

It was during this time that Bible translations in multiple languages were introduced to the common people. Due to the increased access to the Scriptures, the common man began to question the political church practices.

1170 A.D. witnessed the birth of both the Albigenses and the Waldensians in France. Both groups were bitterly persecuted by the Roman church.

Thomas Aquinas (1226-1274) began to establish systematic theological doctrines which are the foundation of many positions still held in the church today.

In 1380 A.D. John Wycliff produced his New Testament in English, and just four years later published the Old Testament in English.

John Huss of Bohemia, the rector of the University of Prague for quite some time, was condemned and burned to death in 1416 A.D. for his preaching of Wycliff's doctrines.

Martin Luther nailed his thesis to the door at Wittenberg in 1479 calling on the Pope to stop his anti-Biblical practices. Just 19 years later Jerome Savonarola having preached against the social, ecclesiastical, and political wickedness of his day was excommunicated by the Pope and ultimately hanged and burned in the public square in Florence.

The strengthening of the access to the Scriptures sparked what is called the Great Reformation, which in essence was a return to the Scriptures as the authority for matters of faith and practice. A great Renaissance of science and exploration followed on its heels with one of the most notable discoveries being the Americas by the Italian explorer Christopher Columbus in 1492 A.D.

Phillip Melanchthon, Martin Luther's understudy, further developed a system of theological studies in his *Loci Communes* in 1521 A.D.

In 1525 A.D. William Tyndale produced his English translation of the Bible, followed by Martin Luther's German Translation in 1534 A.D., and Fransico de Enzinas with his Spanish translation in 1543 A.D. The Swedish *Gusta Vasa* Bible came in 1541 A.D., and the Czech Bible was produced in 1579A.D. The French received their language translation in 1535 A.D. and the Hungarians received theirs in 1590 A.D.

In 1604 A.D., the English version authorized by King James of England was begun as an attempt to get the best possible translation into the English language. Using the Bishops Bible as its base nearly 50 scholars from different universities and ecclesiastical backgrounds set out to produce an acceptable version that would standardize the English translation. It was completed in 1611 A.D. with the provision that there would be periodic updates as needed. We currently use the 1769 edition completed just 7 years before American Independence was declared.

Identifying characteristics:

- Works
- Name that lives but are actually dead
- Strengthen what remains
- Some things are ready to die
- Works are not perfect

- ◆ Some names who have not defiled their garments

- ◆ Some are worthy to walk in white with the Lord

## 6th) The Church of Philadelphia 1750-1975 A.D.

Most of the church age timelines start the church of Philadelphia in 1750 A.D. and end in approximately 1925 A.D. It is hard to pinpoint the exact date. However, the great missionary movements of the past generation seemed to get their start around 1739 A.D. when John Wesley came in contact with the Moravians and then started preaching about the witness of the Spirit. In 1784 A.D. he organized the Methodists in the United States.

It was about this time that George Whitefield began preaching great revival meetings across America. In my personal library I have a copy of John Wesley's eulogy of Whitefield in 1770 A.D. in which he said:

"O God, with thee no word is impossible: thou dost whatsoever pleaseth thee? O that thou wouldst cause the mantle of thy prophet, whom thou hast taken up now to fall upon us that remain! Where is the Lord God of Elijah? Let his spirit rest upon these thy servants Show thou art the God that answerest by fire!"

It seems that his prayer was answered. Revivals continued to sweep the continents. The missionary movement spread the Gospel around the world, and God's support in those endeavors seemed to be limitless.

In 1792 A.D. William Carey preached the now famous sermon "Attempt great things for God and expect great things from God." This led to the organization of the Baptist Missionary Society and ultimately Carey's mission to India.

In 1956 A.D. five young missionaries gave their lives in the Amazon jungle attempting to reach an uncivilized tribe known as the fierce Huaorani Tribe. Their sacrifice served as a platform to enlist hundreds of young people for mission work across the globe.

In 1954 A.D., Dr. Arlin Horton and his wife, Beka, started a Christian school in Pensacola, Florida. Quickly discovering the lack of materials for a Biblically-based education, they began producing their own materials. When others began to see what they were producing they began to ask for materials and A Beka Book publishing company was born. In 1968 my own father, Dr. David R. Haifley, began a Christian school and in the early '70s began using the Horton materials. This Christian School movement trained thousands of young Christians to stand on the front lines for their faith. The effort of the Hortons was followed by several other Christian publishers attempting to fill the need.

Identifying characteristics:

- Works

- An open door that no man could shut

- Has a little strength

- Kept His Word

- Has not denied His name

- Kept from the hour of temptation

- Hold fast what they have


**7th) The Church of Laodicea 1975-present A.D.**

Some have suggested that the Laodicean era started as early as 1881. This would tie its beginning to the publishing of Westcott and Hort's new Greek text and the subsequent Revised Standard Version. Others have placed it in 1925 when the modernist movement got underway, replacing the traditional Creation view with Theistic Evolution and other humanistic ideas.

While these dates have some validity, I would submit that the common era of wealth in the church began in 1975 with the founding of the Willow Creek Community Church in Chicago.

Saddle Back Community Church in California followed suit in 1979 and this began a flood of "new style" churches. The idea promoted by these model churches was to use marketing techniques to attract visitors. They put an emphasis on making "seeker-friendly" churches.

Massive studies were done to find out what would make people come to church, and then strategies were comprised to meet those expectations. Gone was the idea that the Pastor was the mouthpiece of God. Now the church focused on the wants and desires of people, shaping worship to fit what people were comfortable with. Laodicea means just that: the voice of the people.

The pulpit was removed and stages were opened up to accommodate more entertaining musicians. Feelings and emotions began to be stoked. This resulted in an influx of cash. Churches became state of the art. Preachers started buying Cadillacs and beach houses. Parishioners no longer needed to give up their lifestyle. Drinking alcohol became a common practice. Gambling, dancing, and movie shows, prohibited in the previous generation, became commonplace and in some cases became the basis for self-bettering sermons. Restaurants and coffee shops moved into church foyers to round out the new church experience. Immorality, of all kinds, became accepted as the norm. In some cases, it has even become encouraged. The power to change your life has become an elusive idea. Laodicea seems to be described in exactly this way.

**Identifying characteristics:**

- Works that are neither cold nor hot
- Rich and increased with goods have need of nothing
- Spiritually wretched, miserable, poor, blind, naked
- Voice of the people

## -Parallel Kingdom Parables

There are seven parables in Matthew 13 that describe the Kingdom of Christ from seven different perspectives. If you believe, as I do, that the church of Jesus Christ is one and the same as the Kingdom of Jesus Christ then these descriptions are very interesting.

## The Sower and the Seed  Matthew 13:1-23  Ephesus

This period of sowing came in the early church. Literally, every part of the world was given the Gospel. In Colossians 1:23 Paul states that the entire world had received the gospel message in his lifetime. With the aid of the gift of tongues and the sign miracles, the church became visible in all of its glory to everyone. However, as we see in this parable not everyone received it.

## The Wheat and the Tares  Matthew 13:24-30  Smyrna

It was during the Smyrna church period that heretics began to pervert the scriptures. The early church fathers were calling them out even before the scriptures were completely canonized. The letter to the Galatians and the letters to Timothy and Titus are very pointed in their condemnation of the tares that were being sown. One of my favorite quotes in the writings of the Ante-Nicene fathers was of Irenaeus. Reportedly, Marcion who was guilty of cutting much of the gospels and epistles from the inspired scriptures and claiming that Abraham's God and the Christians God were different, came in contact with Irenaeus in a public place. Irenaeus did not acknowledge his existence which made Marcion angry. He confronted Irenaeus saying, "Don't you know who I am." Whereupon Irenaeus replied, "I know who thou art. Thou firstborn son of Satan."

## The Mustard Seed  Matthew 13:31-32  Pergamos

This was the church of Constantine. The little seeds of the gospel which were planted grew into a large tree. It was here that the church became powerful, political, and visible.

### The Leaven  Matthew 13:33  Thyatira

Leaven the picture of sin became hidden in the middle of the Bread of Life. It permeated the church and suddenly the church look more world-like than God-like.

### The Treasure  Matthew 13:44  Sardis

The treasure found during the Sardis church was undoubtedly the Word of God. The Bible was translated into multiple languages, and great reformation swept the globe.

### The Pearl  Matthew 13:45-46  Philadelphia

Not a word of condemnation of this era. Using the Bible as its sword and light, the church of Philadelphia spent its fortune on great missionary efforts. Some of the greatest philanthropy for the cause of Christ is recorded during this time. Borden of Yale, George Mueller, Robert Sheffey, D.L. Moody and Billy Sunday were some names that come to mind.

### The Net  Matthew 13:47-50  Laodicea

A description of the last church filled with good fish and bad is an interesting picture. Verse 49 even mentions the end of the world, and the separation of the good and bad.


## -The Restoration of the Old Covenant Blessings

The Old Testament scriptures are built around seven different covenants between God and man. In each of these covenants, man failed and lost the special thing that God had promised them. In the promises to the overcomers of the seven churches, each one of those lost things was given back.

Edenic covenant—man lost the tree of life and was forbidden to even come near it. Revelation 2:7 gives the tree of life back.

Adamic covenant– man suffers under the curse of death. Revelation 2:11 states that the overcomer will not be hurt with the second death.

Noahic Covenant– man suffers from a complete separation from God's creation and the rest of humankind. Revelation 2:17 gives man a permanent connection with his Creator in the form of food, a stone token, and a new name that establishes a personal relationship.

Abrahamic Covenant– In the rubble of Babel Abraham loses his identification with his nation. He becomes a wanderer and a tent dweller. Revelation 2:26 establishes power over the nations and a ruling position.

Mosaic Covenant– Israel is in such a state that Moses is compelled to argue against God blotting them out from under heaven. In Revelation 3:5 God states that the overcomer will not be blotted out, but will instead be confessed openly in heaven.

Palestinian Covenant– This covenant was about the land of Israel with Jerusalem being the capital of the nation. Israel was dispersed and harried from their land due to their own wickedness. Revelation 3:12 makes the overcomer a pillar in the temple of God and a name put in the city of New Jerusalem.

Davidic Covenant– The promise to David ensured that someone from his lineage would sit on the throne forever. Due to the wickedness of David's posterity, the entire line was cursed to the point that the rightful heir of the throne, Joseph, had to work hard as a carpenter for a living. It is to the overcomers of the Laodicean church in Revelation 3:21 that God grants a place on the Davidic throne.

# Section 3

**Chapter:** Five

**Title:** The Throne Room

**Summary:** Chapters four and five discuss the rapture of the church and the view that we will see immediately following that rapture. In this case, John is our representative. What John sees is what we will see. This is the first look at our Advocate and how He argues our case for redemption.

**Study Outline:**

1.  The Rapture of the Church

2.  The Throne Room

3.  The Book of Redemption

# 5

# The Throne Room

## -The Rapture of the Church

*"After this I looked, and, behold, a door was opened in heaven: and the first voice which I heard was as it were of a trumpet talking with me: which said, Come up hither, and I will shew thee things which must be hereafter. And immediately I was in the spirit; and, behold, a throne was set in heaven, and one sat on the throne." Revelation 4:1-2*

The elements of this verse seem to be echoing the events of what we call, "The Rapture" of the church.

- Heaven is opened

- A trumpet is sounding

- Come up hither is the call

- A transfer to the Spirit world is taking place

- The saint is ushered into the Presence of the Lord

In Paul's writings ( I Thessalonians 4:16-17) we find this same event described this way:

*"For the Lord himself shall descend from heaven with a shout, with the voice of the archangel, and with the trump of God: and the dead in Christ shall rise first: Then we which are alive and remain shall be caught up together with them in the*

*clouds, to meet the Lord in the air: and so shall we ever be with the Lord."*

We call it "The Rapture" because we will be completely enraptured with the event. The Lord will descend, the trump will sound, we will be reunited with those who have gone on before, and then be ushered into the presence of Christ.

Historically, we have Enoch as the first example of a "Raptured" saint. Genesis 5:24 says this, *"And Enoch walked with God: and he was not; for God took him."* We wouldn't know exactly what that meant if wasn't for a subsequent explanation in Hebrews (11:5), *"By faith Enoch was translated that he should not see death; and was not found, because God had translated him..."* Elijah also seems to have been "translated" in a similar manner according to II Kings 2:11. The Bible tells us that he went up by a whirlwind into heaven. These were examples of what the translation of living saints would be like when the Lord returns.

Another interesting reference to this event is found in the Song of Solomon (2:10-13):

> *"My beloved spake, and said unto me, Rise up, my love, my fair one, and come away. For, lo, the winter is past, the rain is over and gone; The flowers appear on the earth; the time of the singing of birds is come, and voice of the turtle is heard in our land; the fig tree putteth forth her green figs, and the vines with the tender grape give a good smell. Arise, my love, my fair one, and come away." Rise, Come away,"* is the call of the Bridegroom to His Bride, the Church.

In each of these cases, the idea of being called up is presented. When this call comes to John in Revelation 4, it is almost as if he is our representative. He seems to be another type of the church being called up, only in this case what he sees after the calling is visible. John is seeing what we will see when we are called up.

## -The Throne Room

It's important to state here again that John saw what we will be seeing in the same way that we will be seeing it. As you read Revelation 4 imagine if you will, that you have just stepped into this magnificent place and your eyes are gradually taking in the scenery.

The first thing he sees is a throne. As his eyes become accustomed to the place, he makes out a Person sitting on the throne. The One on the throne looks like jasper and a sardine stone. The jasper and sardine stone is the color of fire and blood. Around the throne is a rainbow like an emerald. This is reminiscent of the aurora borealis, which we typically call, "The Northern Lights."

He then notices twenty-four elders sitting on seats around the throne. Each of them is clothed in white and is crowned with a golden crown.

Next, he sees that the throne is producing lightning and thunder and voices. Up close around the front of the throne are seven lamps of fire, which, he explains, are the seven Spirits of God.

A massive sea of glass-like crystal seems to engulf the area immediately in front of the throne. The are other descriptions in the Bible of this exact scene. Exodus 24:10 describes it as *"paved work of a sapphire stone, and as it were the body of heaven in his clearness."* Ezekiel seems to have a view from beneath the sea of glass. He speaks of four creatures underneath the throne, and on their heads is a firmament of crystal (Ezekiel 1:22). I can't help but think that what looks like a sky of crystal from underneath looks like a sea of glass from up above. Ezekiel's view is from the earth, while John's view is from a heavenly vantage point. Therefore, one sees a sky the other sees a sea.

John begins to pick up more details in verse six, as he becomes more aware of what is going on around the throne. He sees four beasts in and around the throne. Each beast has a different look.

One looks like a lion, one like a calf, one like a man, and one like a flying eagle. Each beast has six wings and multiple eyes. Their job seems to be specifically proclaiming the Holiness of the Lord God Almighty, and His permanent place in time past, time present, and time future. Interestingly enough, Isaiah 6 describes a similar scene:

> *"In the year that king Uzziah died I saw also the Lord sitting upon a throne, high and lifted up, and his train filled the temple. Above it stood the seraphims: each one had six wings; with twain he covered his face, and with twain he covered his feet, and with twain he did fly. And one cried unto another, and said, Holy, holy, holy, is the LORD of hosts: the whole earth is full of his glory." Isaiah 6:1-3*

When the four beasts give glory to God, the twenty-four elders cast their golden crowns at the foot of the throne and pronounce that the Lord alone is worthy to receive glory and honor and power. It's important to note that these twenty-four elders are mentioned six times throughout Revelation and that the same crowns seem to appear again on the head of Christ in chapter nineteen.

## -The Book of Redemption

In chapter five we read these words:

> *"And I saw in the right hand of him that sat on the throne a book written within and on the backside, sealed with seven seals. And I saw a strong angel proclaiming with a loud voice, Who is worthy to open the book, neither to look thereon. And I wept much, because no man was found worthy to open and the read the book, neither to look thereon." (Rev.5:1-4)*

The idea that there are books in heaven that record everything is not only mentioned in Revelation. Moses and the Lord speak of a book as far back as Exodus 32:-32-33:

> *"Yet now, if thou wilt forgive their sin; and if not, blot me, I pray thee, out of thy book which thou hast written. And the*

In this case, they are discussing blotting out people who are written in the book. I believe this could be the book of Life which is mentioned several other times in scripture.

*"Let them be blotted out of the book of the living, and not be written with the righteous." Psalm 69:28*

*"Thine eyes did see my substance, yet being unperfect; and in thy book all my members were written, which in continuance were fashioned, when as yet there was none of them." Psalm139:16*

*"And all that dwell upon the earth shall worship him, whose names are not written in the book of life of the Lamb slain from the foundation of the world." Rev. 13:8*

*"The beast that thou sawest was, and is not; and shall ascend out of the bottomless pit, and go into perdition: and they that dwell on the earth shall wonder, whose names were not written in the book of life from the foundation of the world, when they behold the beast that was, and is not, and yet is." Rev. 17:8*

*"And I saw the dead, small and great, stand before God; and the books were opened: and another book was opened, which is the book of life: and the dead were judged out of those things which were written in the books, according to their works." Rev. 20:12*

*"And whosoever was not found written in the book of life was cast into the lake of fire." Rev. 20:15*

*"And there shall in no wise enter into it any thing that defileth, neither whatsoever worketh abomination, or maketh a lie: but they which are written in the Lamb's book of life." Rev. 21:27*

All of these verses seem to be referencing a "Book of Life." The book seems to contain all living humans from Adam to the last one. It also appears that some are blotted out and, therefore, in the last judgment they are not found in the book.

There also seems to be a book that records our works.

*"Thou tellest my wanderings: put thou my tears into thy bottle: are they not in thy book?" Psalm 56:8*

*"Then they that feared the LORD spake often one to another: and the LORD hearkened, and heard it, and a book of remembrance was written before him for them that feared the LORD, and that thought upon his name." Mal. 3:16*

*"And I saw the dead, small and great, stand before God; and the books were opened: and another book was opened, which is the book of life: and the dead were judged out of those things which were written in the books, according to their works." Rev. 20:12*

There are other books mentioned as well. Revelation 10 speaks of a book that John is told to take and eat and it will make his belly bitter. A very similar thing is told to Ezekiel only it is called a scroll in the Old Testament. Then Hebrews talks of the "volume of the book," which speaks of Jesus. However, none of these books fit the description of the book mentioned in Revelation five.

This book with the seven seals seems to be one of a kind. Many have tried to explain that this book with seven seals is the unfolding of the Great Tribulation. Is that true? How can we know? To determine what this book is about we must look at every detail surrounding it. The following details may give us a clue as to what it might be about.

- John is weeping because no one can open it. Why is this? If it is a book about the Great Tribulation, why is John so upset that no one can open it. If it is about destruction why does he want to open it so badly?

- No man in heaven, nor in earth is worthy to open the book.

This same idea is mentioned elsewhere in the Bible. *"And I sought for a man among them that should make up the hedge, and stand in the gap before me for the land, that I should not destroy it: but I found none."* Ezekiel 22:30 And then again, *"And he saw that there was no man, and wondered that there was no intercessor...."* Isaiah 59:16 *"For I beheld, and there was no man; even among them, and there was no counsellor, that, when I asked of them, could answer a word."* Isaiah 41:28 In these three verses the problem of salvation is being addressed. Man is in dire straights and no man can bridge the gap. There is no one worthy to fix the brokenness between us and the Father. This book must have something to do with this topic.

- The only One who can open these seals also happens to be the only One who can speak to the Father for us. *"And one of the elders saith unto me, Weep not: behold, the Lion of the tribe of Juda, the Root of David, hath prevailed to open the book, and to loose the seven seals thereof. And I beheld, and lo, in the midst of the throne and of the four beasts, and in the midst of the elders, stood a Lamb as it had been slain, having seven horns and seven eyes, which are the seven Spirits of God sent forth into all the earth. And he came and took the book out of the right hand of him that sat upon the throne."* Revelation 5:5-7 Only the Lamb could open the seals. When it comes to salvation the scriptures are clear, there is only One who can save us. Isaiah tells us that when God looked for an intercessor He couldn't find one. Therefore He put on His armor and brought deliverance by Himself (Isa 59:16-19). I Timothy 2:5 points us towards this same idea: *"For there is one God, and one mediator between God and men, the man Christ Jesus."* Is it possible that these verses are all talking about the same thing? Is this book about our Salvation? Is this book the story of our Redemption?

- The opening of the book results in the song of the Redeemed praising the Lamb for being slain and redeeming us to God making us kings and priests.

- The opening of the book results in the Angels praising the Lamb that was slain. Their song is this: "Worthy is the Lamb that was slain to receive power, and riches, and wisdom, and strength, and honour, and glory, and blessing."

- The opening of the book results in the praise of every creature on earth and under the earth, and those that are in the sea. They are found blessing the One on the throne and the Lamb.

- The opening of the book results in the twenty-four elders falling down and worshipping "Him that liveth for ever and ever."

- The spirit of the scene is not one of horror at the destruction, but one of rejoicing and praise to the Lamb.

As I have pondered these facts coupled with other scriptures I have come to the conclusion that this is the moment when our Advocate (I John 2:1-2) argues the case of our redemption before the Almighty as well as the entire Universe of living beings. **The book with the seven seals, then, is the story of mankind, his fall, and his redemption.** Only the seventh seal covers the final years which we call the Great Tribulation. We will attempt to prove this theory in the next chapter.

**Chapter:** Six

**Title:** The Sealed Book

**Summary:** The first six seals tell the story of mankind up to the current events happening in chapters four and five. The seventh seal marks a change in the narrative in chapter eight and will, therefore, be dealt with in a separate chapter.

**Study Outline:**

1.  The Four Horsemen

2.  The Fifth Seal

3.  The Sixth Seal

# The Sealed Book

**6**

What is this sealed book? Why is it sealed? It was common in the kingdoms which existed during Bible times for a document to be sealed by a king. Only those who had the proper authorization could open the seals. If a book had multiple seals, typically, it meant that different people had the authorization to open different parts of the book. In this case, we find that no one could be found in heaven or on earth to open the document. John is weeping because no one can be found to open it. Why is he weeping? Is it because this book contains the information that declares our redemption? Is it the sealed copy of our inheritance?

Indeed, this sealed book seems to be the book that describes the fall and redemption of mankind. Our Advocate is the only one who can loose the seals and tell the story. It seems He is literally defending our right to be in this magnificent place. You will find in Revelation 19:8 that His expert testimony results in the granting of white robes to the redeemed. So then, Revelation chapter six through the first part of chapter nineteen could be our defense before the Almighty. If we look at this sealed book in this way it begins to make a little more sense than just a narrative of multiple judgments.

It is important to see the distinction between the first six seals and the seventh one. The first six are all revealed in one chapter

(Revelation 6). Chapter seven then is the result of the first six and is intrinsically connected to them. When we get to chapter eight a distinct difference is marked by the statement in verse one, *"And when he had opened the seventh seal, there was silence in heaven about the space of half an hour."* This indicates that there is a change in perspective coming. We will revisit this in the next chapter.

## -The Four Horsemen

Let's begin the study of this story of redemption by looking at the four horsemen. They are unique and separated from the other seals by their unique presentation. I must remind the reader that the fanciful interpretations of the "Four Horsemen of the Apocalypse" are a gross misunderstanding of what they really represent. Remember that "Apocalypse" means "Revelation." It does not mean "End Time Judgement."

Some have tried to tie the rider of the first horse with the Anti-Christ or Beast of Revelation thirteen. Some would say that these four horses should be feared as the harbingers of judgment. Just who are they and what do they mean? May I suggest that we look at them in the context of what we have learned about the book as it pertains to our redemption? Is it possible that they are actually a presentation of the story of mankind?

Dr. William Milligan, professor of Divinity and Biblical Criticism at the university of Aberdeen, writes in the 1895 edition of the Expositors Bible:

> "Probably it is enough to say that not one of the four riders is a person. Each is rather a cause, a manifestation of certain truths connected with the kingdom of Christ..."

Could the professor be correct? Are these representatives of something moving through the earth in the lives of men?

It is interesting to note that these four distinct colors of horses appear in the prophecy of Zechariah 6:2-5. Their behavior and activity parallel what we learn about them in Revelation.

*"And I turned, and lifted up mine eyes, and looked, and, behold, there came four chariots out from between two mountains; and the mountains were mountains of brass, In the first chariot were red horses; and in the second chariot black horses; And in the third chariot white horses; and in the fourth chariot grisled and bay horses. Then I answered and said unto the angel that talked with me, What are these, my lord? And the angel answered and said unto me, These are the four spirits of the heavens, which go forth from standing before the Lord of all the earth."*

Then Zechariah (6:7) goes on to tell us this interesting fact:

*"And the bay went forth, and sought to go that they might walk to and from through the earth: and he said, Get you hence, walk to and fro through the earth. So they walked to and from through the earth."*

So they seem to have been sent from the throne, and they seem to be moving about on the earth. Is it possible that this "to and fro" is a reference to them moving about in time, even as Job describes the actions of Satan?

Let's follow that line of thinking and see where it leads us.

**The White Horse**

The color is important or it would not have been mentioned. It is white. Professor Milligan makes this comment about the color:

"The color of the horse is white, for throughout these visions that color is always the symbol of heavenly purity:"

I concur with the opinion of the learned professor. White is always a symbol of purity and even more so in this book of Revelation. Notice this reference in Revelation 19:8: *" And to her was granted that she should be arrayed in fine linen, clean and white: for the fine linen is the righteousness of saints."* We don't need to do a deep dive study of the Biblical color white at this point because, truly, white is universally accepted as representing purity. This then would mean that the spirit represented by this horse must be one of purity. It couldn't possibly be a reflection of the Anti-Christ beast.

We see then that there is someone on the horse, and he is given both a bow and a crown. His activity and goal is to conquer. Who could this be? Is it possible that this is the beginning of the story of mankind? Let's go back to Genesis and see if there are any parallels.

First, we see in Genesis 1:27 that God created man in his own image. Of course, man began his life purely in the image of God. He had not sinned at this point and was placed in the Garden of Eden. We often call this the Dispensation (or Age) of Innocence. It might better be termed the Age of Purity, even though it was short lived. We actually don't know how long Adam and Eve were in the Garden of Eden. Because of the brevity of the account we naturally assume it was days or even hours. Some mathematicians have suggested that it could have been as long as 150 years. We have no way of knowing.

The charge to Adam is interesting in that it includes a clause about dominion which would point back to the crown on our white horse rider. Man was given the world in his pure state and was given power (the bow) and authority (the crown) to rule over the creation. When the flood destroyed the earth the charge given to Noah and his family, the only remaining humans, was almost identical to the one given to Adam. *"....Be fruitful, and multiply, and replenish the earth. And the fear of you and the dread of you shall be upon every beast of the earth, and upon every fowl of the air, upon all that moveth upon the earth, and upon all the fishes of the sea; into your hand are they delivered."*

The command to conquer and have dominion has not changed at all. We are still given the responsibility to tame and rule this earth. It is a moving horse, moving "to and fro" in the earth. The horse moves through continents and time in the same manner.

So then this White Horse is the representation of Man in his purist state with the edict of heaven on him to conquer and subdue the earth.

## The Red Horse

If, indeed, the white horse is the beginning and continuation of man's story, than the red horse is story of man's fall and the subsequent death of the sinner.

Power is given to this rider to take peace from the earth. Killing is introduced and a sword is the symbol of this spirit. There never has been peace on the earth since the Garden of Eden. When man fell, the sentence of death was pronounced on him. By Genesis chapter four man is killing man. The red blood is crying from the ground. In the post-diluvian covenant with Noah we find the continued problem with killing. *"And surely your blood of your lives will I require; at the hand of every beast will I require it, and the hand of man; at the hand of every man's brother will I require the life of man. Whoso sheddeth man's blood, by man shall his blood be shed; for in the image of God made he man."* (Gen. 9:5-6).

History goes on to record "wars and rumors of wars." A constant epic drama of man killing man throughout the entire period of man's existence.

## The Black Horse

Three things are identified with this horse and rider. The first is a pair of balances. This seems to be pointing towards a measuring of something. Looking through the Bible we find these verses:

*"Your iniquities, and the iniquities of your fathers together, saith the LORD, which have burned incense upon the mountains, and blasphemed me upon the hills: therefore will I measure their former work into their bosom"* Isaiah 65:7

*"O thou that dwellest upon many waters, abundant in treasures,*

*thine end is come, and the measure of thy covetousness." Jeremiah 51:13*

*"The way of the just is uprightness: thou, most upright, dost weigh the path of the just." Isaiah 26:7*

*"And thou, son of man, take thee a sharp knife, take thee a barber's razor, and cause it to pass upon thine head and upon thy beard: then take thee balances to weigh, and divide the hair." Ezekiel 5:1*

*"Talk no more so exceeding proudly; let not arrogancy come out of your mouth: for the LORD is a God of knowledge, and by him actions are weighed." 1Samuel 2:3*

*"Oh that my grief were throughly weighed, and my calamity laid in the balances together!" Job 6:2*

*"Let me be weighed in an even balance, that God may know mine integrity." Job 31:6*

*"TEKEL; Thou art weighed in the balances, and art found wanting." Daniel 5:27*

Each one of these verses demonstrates that God is weighing the hearts and minds of mankind. The last reference found in Daniel is a prophetic reference to the end of the Babylonian king. It is the clearest picture of the balances that are being used to measure the hearts and minds of mankind and demonstrates the New Testament verse which says, *"For all have sinned, and come short of the glory of God." Romans 3:23* We are all being measured by God and all of us have been found wanting.

The second thing identified by this horse is found in the voice heard coming from the middle of the four beasts around the throne (Rev. 6:6), *"And I heard a voice in the midst of the four beasts say, A measure of wheat for a penny, and three measures of barley for a penny;..."* (We will deal with the rest of the phase in a little bit.) Because this voice is coming from the midst of the four beasts we must assume it is coming from the one who is sitting on the throne, The Eternal Christ, Himself. What does it mean?

Some have suggested that it is a reference to a famine that will come on the earth. This conclusion is arrived at because of the assumption that the price of the food is being described as inexpensive. However, I would like to suggest that a famine is not what is being described here. In fact, it might just be the exact opposite of a famine.

A very similar phrase is found in an Old Testament story:

*"Then Elisha said, Hear ye the word of the Lord; Thus saith the Lord, To morrow about this time shall a measure of fine flour be sold for a shekel, and two measures of barley for a shekel, in the gate of Samaria." II Kings 7:1*

There had been a famine in Samaria because of a siege by the king of Syria. II Kings 6:25 tells us that the situation was so dire that an ass's head was sold for eighty pieces of silver and a quarter of a cab of dove's dung was sold for five pieces of silver. The verse above follows this moment. Elisha tells the king that the situation is going to be immediately better by the next day. He states that the blessing of God is coming and food will be available at a more than affordable rate.

I would like to submit to you that this verse in Revelation 6:6 is a description of the blessing of the Lord. Throughout scripture, the concept is taught that the Lord gives blessing to all...even those who don't believe on Him. Consider these verses in this context:

*"That ye may be the children of your Father which is in heaven: for he maketh his sun to rise on the evil and on the good, and sendeth rain on the just and on the unjust." Matthew 5:45*

*"Neither is worshipped with men's hands, as though he needed any thing, seeing he giveth to all life, and breath, and all things;" Acts 17:25*

*"Who giveth food to all flesh: for his mercy endureth for ever."*

*"Charge them that are rich in this world, that they be not high-minded, nor trust in uncertain riches, but in the living God, who giveth us richly all things to enjoy;" 1Timothy 6:17*

*" If any of you lack wisdom, let him ask of God, that giveth to all men liberally, and upbraideth not; and it shall be given him." James 1:5*

Is it possible that this rider of the black horse is actually measuring what man does with the blessings of God? This would fit into the idea that this is the story of man. Once again we are reminded that man comes short of the Glory of God. We are measured and found wanting, just like Belteshazzar of Babylon.

The third thing identified by this horse,  is the protected status of the oil and wine. *"...and see thou hurt not the oil and wine."* What is this about?

Thirty-six verses in the Old Testament put oil and wine together. In most of these cases, it is a reference to a sacrifice. Here are some examples of those verses:

*"And with the one lamb a tenth deal of flour mingled with the fourth part of an hin of beaten oil; and the fourth part of an hin of wine for a drink offering." Exodus 29:40*

*"And the meat offering thereof shall be two tenth deals of fine flour mingled with oil, an offering made by fire unto the LORD for a sweet savour: and the drink offering thereof shall be of wine, the fourth part of an hin." Leviticus 23:13*

*"All the best of the oil, and all the best of the wine, and of the wheat, the firstfruits of them which they shall offer unto the LORD, them have I given thee." Numbers 18:12*

If the rider of the black horse is weighing the hearts and minds of mankind, and if he is considering the blessings of God on them, they will all be found wanting. All will be condemned. But is all of mankind condemned? Remember Romans 4:3, *"For what saith the scripture? Abraham believed God, and it was coundted unto him for righteousness."* And consider Hebrews 11 which says, *"By faith Abel...By faith Enoch...By faith Noah...By faith Abraham...By faith Isaac...By faith Jacob...By faith Joseph..."* and so on. These people found grace in God's sight by faith. Even though they were weighed and found wanting, through the substitutionary sacrifice, they were not condemned. These saints will be seen again in the fifth seal. They escaped the judgement brought by the Pale horse because of the sacrifice represented by the oil and wine. The rider was instructed not to hurt them because they were protected.

**The Pale Horse**

Death and Hell are the natural consequence of being weighed in the balances and found wanting. *"For the wages of sin is death;"* the Apostle Paul reminds us in Romans six.

Why do some folks die young? Why do some die of hunger and some in tragic events? There is no way for us to know the specific reasons for each tragic death but Revelation 6:8 indicates that Death and Hell are given specific power to kill one fourth of the world. Four different types of death are recorded: *"With sword"* (military deaths), *"with hunger"* (famine), *"with death"* (random tragic reasons), and *"with the beasts of the earth"* (death by animals). My assumption, based on this description is that these deaths are not the normal deaths that come at the end of a long life but are rather sudden and inexplicable. This power is given to these two as a direct result of the sin of mankind and our failure to balance the scales of justice.


## -The Fifth Seal

To understand the fifth seal in the way we present it, you must see the four horsemen as consecutive and each new one a consequence of the one before. If mankind in his intended role is represented on the first horse, the second horse represents the fall and subsequent violence permeating the earth, the third horse continues through time weighing and measuring what man does with the blessings of God, and the fourth horse is the result of man's failure to measure up, then the fifth seal is the holding place for those who trusted by faith and were kept in a safe place until the time of the crucifixion when the Lamb was sacrificed to pay for their sins. Notice what Revelation states about this fifth seal:

> *"And when he had opened the fifth seal, I saw under the altar the souls of them that were slain for the word of God, and for the testimony which they held: And they cried with a loud voice, saying, How long, O Lord, holy and true, dost thou not judge and avenge our blood on them that dwell on the earth? And white robes were given unto every one of them; and it was said unto them, that they should rest yet for a little season, until their fellowservants also and their brethren, that should be killed as they were, should be fulfilled." Revelation 6:9-11*

The cry of these saints is one of vengeance. Nothing is said about a Lamb at this point. In fact, it appears that they are unfamiliar with the concept of the Lamb. They were faithful on earth. They worshipped the Lord who is holy and true. Their prayer is an Old Testament prayer, much like the ones David prayed which are recorded for us in the book of Psalms. I am reminded of the time Jesus stood up in the temple and read from Isaiah 61. He read the first part of the prophecy in verse 2 *"To proclaim the acceptable year of the LORD."* He stopped in the middle of the verse and put a period where Isaiah had put a comma. The folks in the synagogue that day were stunned when He didn't finish the reading. All of their attention was fixed on Him because He had left off this part: *"and the day of vengeance of our God."* That Old Testament righteous indignation of Jonah didn't seem to go away after their death. They are impatient and ask the Lord "How long do we have to wait?" until the end.

Knowing that no prophecy of the scripture stands alone, we immediately search to see if there is a reference to this holding place in any other scriptures. Yes, there is. Consider these following verses in this context:

*"And it came to pass, that the beggar died, and was carried by the angels into Abraham's bosom: the rich man also died, and was buried; And in hell he lift up his eyes, being in torments, and seeth Abraham afar off, and Lazarus in his bosom. And he cried and said, Father Abraham, have mercy on me, and send Lazarus, that he may dip the tip of his finger in water, and cool my tongue; for I am tormented in this flame. But Abraham said, Son, remember that thou in thy lifetime receivedst thy good things, and likewise Lazarus evil things: but now he is comforted, and thou art tormented. And beside all this, between us and you there is a great gulf fixed: so that they which would pass from hence to you cannot; neither can they pass to us, that would come from thence." Luke 16:22-26*

You can read the rest of the story for yourself, but it is obvious that there was a holding place in the heart of the earth for both saints and sinners. They could talk to each other even though they could not cross from one side to another. Jesus called this place "Paradise" when He was on the cross.

*"And Jesus said unto him, Verily I say unto thee, To day shalt thou be with me in paradise." Luke 23:43*

Peter refers to it as a prison and claims that Jesus went there to preach to the souls after His crucifixion.

*"By which also he went and preached unto the spirits in prison;" 1Peter 3:19*

In the book of Ephesians Paul indicates that at this time Jesus led them out of this captive place into the presence of God. After the crucifixion, Paul says Paradise is up not down, and he also says that absence from the body is immediate presence with the Lord. So, then, this place was a temporary holding place for the souls of those who had sacrificed and believed ("hurt not the oil and the wine").

The fifth seal then tells us what happened to those who believed in the Old Testament until the crucifixion. Remember, they don't say anything about the Lamb at this point. This is important because everyone else in the story is praising the Lamb, but not these folks. It was not until Jesus preached to them, that they understood it. They were to wait until something happened. Not to get ahead of the story, but I must point your attention to something. Chapter seven finds everyone rejoicing about salvation and the Lamb. This doesn't happen until seal six is opened.

## -The Sixth Seal

The sixth seal is often confused with the prophecy Jesus made in Matthew 24:29 which speaks of the sun being darkened and the moon not giving her light. That prophecy is fulfilled after the tribulation not during it. Jesus clearly says this:

*"Immediately after the tribulation of those days shall the sun be darkened, and the moon shall not give her light, and the stars shall fall from heaven, and the powers of the heavens shall be shaken:" Matthew 24:29*

So what is this seal? How does it fit with the seals that preceded it?

First look at the context. Immediately following the sixth seal we have a period where the servants of God are sealed. The servants of God before the sixth seal are saying *"How Long....dost thou not judge and avenge..?"* However, those we find in chapter seven have changed their tune. They are saying, *"Salvation to our God which sitteth upon the throne, and unto the Lamb."* The angel in chapter seven verse fourteen says of these sealed servants, *"These are they which came out of great tribulation, and have washed their robes, and made them white in the blood of the Lamb."* The conversation and the praise have changed from seal five to chapter seven. It is a logical assumption that the catalyst for the change is whatever happened in seal six and whatever happened in the first part of chapter seven.

Let's see what happened in seal six. Is there any clue as to what it is about? Can we find this anywhere else in scripture?

The first thing mentioned is a great earthquake followed by the Sun becoming black and the moon turning to the color of blood. The prophet Joel mentioned this time. He said it was before the great and terrible day of the Lord. He also said that after this event happened whosoever would call on the name of the Lord would be delivered.

*"The sun shall be turned into darkness, and moon into blood, before the great and the terrible day of the LORD come. And it shall come to pass, that whosoever shall call on the name of the LORD shall be delivered:..." Joel 2:31-32*

The apostle Peter quoted Joel in Acts 2 on the day of Pentecost. He said that what the people in Jerusalem had just witnessed was a fulfillment of Joel's prophecy. Notice his comment on this:

*"But this is that which was spoken by the prophet Joel; And it shall come to pass in the last days, saith God, I will pour out of my Spirit upon all flesh...And I will shew wonders in heaven above, and signs in the earth beneath; blood, and fire, and vapour of smoke: The sun shall be turned into darkness , and the moon into blood, before that great and notable day of the Lord come: And it shall come to pass, that whosoever shall call on the name of the Lord shall be saved." Acts 2:16-21*

This appears to be a time before the day of the Lord comes. The moon is specifically turned to blood. There are other prophecies that talk about the end time when the sun and moon will be dark. Joel's prophecy mentions this earlier in chapter two verse ten. That time is also the one referenced by Christ in Matthew 24:29. The moon turning to blood is a very specific prophecy and a very exact reference. Why did Peter say that those who were listening to him at Pentecost had witnessed this event prophesied by Joel? Three thousand people responded to his message and called on the name of the Lord to be saved, exactly as the prophesy had said. Something convinced them. Is it possible that they had actually seen the moon turn to blood?

If you compare the story of the crucifixion to the account of the sixth seal you will see some similarities:

- Moon turned to blood    Acts 2:16-21 / Revelation 6:12

- Darkness over all the land    Matthew 27:45/ Revelation 6:12

- Earthquake and rocks rent  Matthew 27:51/ Revelation 6:12

- General fear    Matthew 27:54, Luke 23:48/ Revelation 6:15

Consider the heavens rolled together like a scroll. Job 9:8 says this about the heavens:

*"Which alone spreadeth out the heavens, and treadeth upon the waves of the sea."*

When the hands of the Creator were nailed to the cross, who was spreading out the heavens? Can I remind you that the Crucifixion was a universal event? When we look at the cataclysmic nature of the death of the Son of God and consider the view from God's perspective, Seal six looks a lot like that moment in time when all the universe was shaken to the core, and the Son of God was brutally crucified on a cruel Roman cross.

It is short sited to view the crucifixion of Jesus as a local event completely ignored by the remainder of the creation. Indeed, if you believe in a worldwide flood, it is not hard to imagine a worldwide cataclysmic event at the passion of Christ. Revelation 7:1-2 speaks of four angels who seem to be ready to bring vengeance on the earth as a result of the events of the sixth seal. They are told to stand down and it appears that they are put in holding under the river Euphrates until the sixth trumpet of the tribulation sounds (Rev. 9:13-15). When they are finally released they bring vengeance without mercy.

The story does not advance to the seventh seal of the book until the servants of God are sealed in their foreheads. This all happens in Chapter seven and I would like us to consider the fact that the events of chapter seven are an immediate response to the events of seals six. If seal six is the heavenly perspective of the crucifixion, then chapter seven is an accounting of the souls that were sealed as a result of it.

What is the seal on their foreheads? Consider the following verses which deal with a sealing of believers:

*"Who hath also sealed us, and given the earnest of the Spirit in our hearts." 2 Corinthians 1:22*

*"In whom ye also trusted, after that ye heard the word of truth, the gospel of your salvation: in whom also after that ye believed, ye were sealed with that holy Spirit of promise," Ephesians 1:13*

*"And grieve not the holy Spirit of God, whereby ye are sealed unto the day of redemption." Ephesians 4:30*

Is it possible that the sealing of believers which comes after we have trusted Christ is the seal that is being referenced in Revelation chapter seven? If that is true, then who are the 144,000 Jews who are sealed? Let's see if we can find out.

**The 144,000**

First, you must notice that two groups are mentioned as being sealed. The 144,000 Jews are the first group sealed in Revelation 7:4-8. In 7:9 we find a second group which is a multitude that can not be numbered of all nations, kindreds, people, and tongues. Both groups appear to be gathered around the throne with one voice declaring, *"Salvation to our God which sitteth upon the throne, and unto the Lamb."* When John is questioned about who these people are he responds with something akin to "You tell me." Whereupon, the elder speaking with him says, *"These ... have washed their robes, and made them white in the blood of the Lamb."* I purposely left out the phrase about great tribulation because I wanted to draw your attention to the part about the white robes washed in the blood of the Lamb. This is the same group we find in Revelation 19:7-8:

> *"Let us be glad and rejoice, and give honour to him: for the marriage of the Lamb is come, and his wife hath made herself ready. And to her was granted that she should be arrayed in fine linen, clean and white: for the fine linen is the righteousness of saints."*

This group is identified with the same language as those people who after the Tribulation are part of the New Jerusalem. Compare these phases:

> *(7:16) "...and he that sitteth on the throne shall dwell among them"*

> *(21:3) "...and God himself shall be with them, and be their God."*

> *(7:17) "...and God shall wipe away all tears from their eyes."*

> *(21:4) "And God shall wipe away all tears from their eyes;"*

> *(7:17) "For the Lamb which is in the midst of the throne shall feed them, and shall lead them unto living fountains of waters:"*

> *(21:6) "...I will give unto him that is athirst of the fountain of the water of life freely."*

Is it possible that it is the same group? That is, both groups are redeemed from the earth. Both groups are those who are sealed after they believed. That would make them part of the church.

Then what is the significance of the 144,000? To answer that question we must look at what identifies them. Before we jump to conclusions we should list the things that we know about them.

Maybe that will help us figure out who they are.

1. They come from all the tribes of the children of Israel. Don't forget that Israel has an everlasting covenant with God. He promises that He will remember them. *"When thou shalt beget children, and children's children, and ye shall have remained long in the land, and shall corrupt yourselves, and make a graven image, or the likeness of any thing, and shall do evil in the sight of the LORD thy God, to provoke him to anger: I call heaven and earth to witness against you this day, that ye shall soon utterly perish from off the land whereunto ye go over Jordan to possess it; ye shall not prolong your days upon it, but shall utterly be destroyed. And the LORD shall scatter you among the nations, and ye shall be left few in number among the heathen, whither the LORD shall lead you. And there ye shall serve gods, the work of men's hands, wood and stone, which neither see, nor hear, nor eat, nor smell. But if from thence thou shalt seek the LORD thy God, thou shalt find him, if thou seek him with all thy heart and with all thy soul. When thou art in tribulation, and all these things are come upon thee, even in the latter days, if thou turn to the LORD thy God, and shalt be obedient unto his voice; (For the LORD thy God is a merciful God;) he will not forsake thee, neither destroy thee, nor forget the covenant of thy fathers which he sware unto them." Deuteronomy 4:25-31*

2. Juda is the first tribe mentioned. This fact connects this group of Jews with the Lion of the Tribe of Juda in Revelation 5:5. He is the only one that can open the seal. The sealing of the 144,000 is not a random part of the story but is intrinsically bound to the story of the book with seven seals.

3. The tribe of Dan is missing. Dan means Judge. It is of particular interest that the judgment tribe is missing.

4. These are the first servants of God to be sealed. The group to follow is one which no man can number of all nations. But this group is specifically Israel.

5. They are mentioned again in Revelation 14:1-5 where we find them standing on Mt. Zion with the Lamb. Where is Mt. Sion (Zion)? I think you might find this quote from the Encyclopedia Britannica to be interesting:

> "In the Old Testament, Zion is overwhelmingly a poetic and prophetic designation and is infrequently used in ordinary prose. It usually has emotional and religious overtones, but it is not clear why the name Zion rather than the name Jerusalem should carry these overtones. The religious and emotional qualities of the name arise from the importance of Jerusalem as the royal city and the city of the Temple. Mount Zion is the place where Yahweh, the God of Israel, dwells (Isaiah 8:18; Psalm 74:2), the place where he is king (Isaiah 24:23) and, where he has installed his king, David (Psalm 2:6). It is thus the seat of the action of Yahweh in history."

So we may not be speaking here of a specific earthly place, but a place with spiritual significance to our Saviour.

6. They sing a new song that they alone can sing (Rev. 14:3). It's important to note that this group of Jewish believers is singled out as having a unique relationship with Christ. Their worship is different than anyone else on earth. No one else can sing their song.

7. They are defined as virgins. Remember that this is a prophetical book and fornication and adultery are spoken of in a spiritual context. Is it possible that virginity is also speaking in a spiritual context? Did you know that Israel is called the "virgin bride" of Jehovah?

> *"Again I will build thee, and thou shalt be built, O virgin of Israel: thou shalt again be adorned with thy tabrets, and shalt go forth in the dances of them that make merry." Jeremiah 31:4*

8. Rev. 14:4 states, *"...These are they which follow the Lamb withersoever he goeth."* This begs the question: "Where is He going and how are they following Him?"

9. *"These were redeemed from among men..."* So this means they are not some superhuman, half angel group of people. They are indeed part of the redeemed.

10. *"...Being the firstfruits unto God and to the Lamb."* (Rev. 14:4) So they are the first fruits. That is specifically talking about the first fruit in a harvest. Hmmm. James 1:18 which was written to the twelve tribes which are scattered abroad says this, *"...that we should be a kind of firstfruits of his creatures."* Another verse comes to mind which uses the same word: *"But now is Christ risen from the dead, and become the firstfruits of them that slept."* I *Cor.15:20* I have to mention the harvest mentioned by Christ to His disciples in John 4:35-38, *"Say not ye, There are yet four months, and then cometh harvest? behold, I say unto you, Lift up your eyes, and look on the fields; for they are white already to harvest. And he that reapeth receiveth wages, and gathereth fruit unto life eternal: that both he that soweth and he that reapeth may rejoice together. And herein is that saying true, One soweth, and another reapeth. I sent you to reap that whereon ye bestowed no labour: other men laboured, and ye are entered into their labours."* Jesus is specifically talking about a harvest in this case. He is telling the disciples that He will be sending them to reap in the harvest. The indication is that they will be the first ones in the field, which would follow that they are reaping the first fruits.

11. They are without guile, and without fault before the throne. Where is this mentioned anywhere else in scripture? The "without guile" comment is unique. Do you remember what Jesus said of Nathaniel? *"Jesus saw Nathanael coming to him, and saith of him, Behold an Israelite indeed, in whom is no guile!"* John 1:47

12. And the most significant fact about them is their specific number. There are 144,000 of them. I would like to point out a couple of things about the number. First of all, you will find that the Lord deals in specific numbers with the Jews. Daniel knew according to the prophet Jeremiah's writings just about when the captivity in Babylon would end. He foretold the exact year when

the Messiah would come to Jerusalem. Revelation eleven speaks of measuring the temple (Ezekiel speaks of the same). Yet when our attention is turned to the outside court, the Gentile court, there are no specific numbers. Days, months, years, Passover, Jubilee, Pentecost all of these were specific and exact numbers.

Now lets turn to the account in Acts of the first fruit harvest of souls. Interestingly enough we are given numbers.

*"Then they that gladly received his word were baptized: and the same day there were added unto them about three thousand souls." Acts 2:41*

Two chapters later we are given another specific number:

*"Howbeit, many of them which heard the word believed; and the number of the men was about five thousand" Acts 4:4*

Then in Acts 6:7, we find this statement:

*"And the word of God increased; and number of the disciples multiplied in Jerusalem greatly; and a great company of the priests were obedient to the faith."*

So the exact numbers that we have recorded of the new believers were all part of virgin Israel. There were 8,000. This number didn't mean anything to me at first until I considered that maybe this was a part of the 144,000. 8,000 multiplied by 18 comes to 144,000. Is this significant? Well, 18 is a significant number for the Jewish people. I would like to give you an exact quote from a Jewish website (shiva.com):

In Judaism, the word "chai" is numerically significant and the number 18 is universally synonymous with this word. Numerically, the word consists of the eighth (8th) and tenth (10th) letters of the Hebrew alphabet Chet (ח)and Yud ,(י)adding up to eighteen the number 18, which is also the word "Chai". According to Jewish traditions and scriptures there are prayers, including the Amidah, commonly referred to as "Shmoneh Esreh" (which translates to "the 18") and refers to the eighteen individual prayers. There is a deep connection drawn upon the word 'chai', its meaning 'life' and the numerical value of the letters that comprise this word.

Traditionally, the Jewish religion, similar to many other religions and cultures, place an emphasis on the significance of life. As such, the literal translation of the word "chai' to 'life is meaningful on its face. In addition, individuals who observe Judaism or identify with the religion are generally guided by basic principles which include characteristics such as kindness, thoughtfulness, selflessness and remaining good natured, both morally and ethically during life on Earth. In addition to the number 18 or numerical significance, the "Chai" is a recognizable symbol commonly worn on necklaces and engraved on rings.

In Judaism, it is common to give and receive gifts in multiples of $18 or "Chai", which in part signifies a good omen for life. In fact, the longstanding Jewish tradition of gifting, contributing or donating in increments of $18 to individuals is often considered a good deed and mitzvah. Generally, these gifting rituals take place in connection with the celebration, honoring or remembrance of loved ones. This custom is also common during all life-cycle events, including rites of passage, and any Jewish occasion from birth announcements and weddings to expressing condolences. The act of giving, gifting or donating $18 or a multiples thereof is commonly referred to as "giving chai." This nomenclature extends to multiples as the number 36 is commonly referred to as "double Chai." Symbolically, these gestures are representative of giving a gift of "life."

Ok...so did you read that? It appears that 18 is the numerical value for a specific Jewish word that means "LIFE." Follow me for a second. If we take the number 8,000 and we give it the "breath of life" (18) we then have the number 144,000. That appears to me to be too coincidental to be coincidental. What if this is the fulfillment of the prophecy of Ezekiel? Read these verses in this context:

> *"Then said he unto me, Prophesy unto the wind, prophesy, son of man, and say to the wind, Thus saith the Lord GOD; Come from the four winds, O breath, and breathe upon these slain, that they may live. So I prophesied as he commanded me, and the breath came into them, and they lived, and stood up upon their feet, an exceeding great army. Then he said unto me, Son of man, these bones are the whole house of Israel: behold, they say, Our bones are dried, and our hope is lost: we are cut off for our parts." Ezekiel 37:9-11*

You can read the rest of the passage on your own. However, isn't it interesting that breath and life are given to the dry bones of Israel and it stands up and begins prophesying? What if these 144,000 are the first Christians in the church? Is this why some of the sign gifts which were so prevalent in the early church have not been visible for 1900 years? Were these early Christians many who had followed the Lord wherever He went (Acts 1:21)? Go back through the list of things we know about them and see if each thing doesn't fit the first Jewish believers.

In summary, if the sixth seal is the crucifixion then chapter seven is the body of believers from Pentecost until the end. This would be the group some would call the "Universal Church," or "The Body of Christ."

**Chapter:** Seven

**Title:** The Seventh Seal

**Summary:** The story of this seal begins in Revelation 8. It is set apart from the rest of the seals by about a half hour of silence in heaven. This seal seems to come to an end four different times. The final view in Revelation 19 shows us the King of Kings bringing us with Him to set up His kingdom on earth.

**Study Outline:**

1. The Four different accounts

2. The Four different views of Christ

3. The Four views of the Tribulation

# The Seventh Seal

Revelation chapter eight begins with an interesting statement:

*"And when he had opened the seventh seal, there was silence in heaven about the space of half an hour." Revelation 8:1*

There seems to be a change in the atmosphere of heaven at this point. From chapter five through chapter seven, while the first six seals are being opened, there is a time of rejoicing and praise. However, a change has come over the entire throne room as they watch what is about to transpire. Jeremiah explains that the judgment of God puts the people of God to silence:

*"Why do we sit still? assemble yourselves, and let us enter into the defenced cities, and let us be silent there: **for the LORD our God hath put us to silence,** and given us water of gall to drink, because we have sinned against the LORD. We looked for peace, but no good came; and for a time of health, and behold trouble! The snorting of his horses was heard from Dan: the whole land trembled at the sound of the neighing of his strong ones; for they are come, and have devoured the land, and all that is in it; the city, and those that dwell therein. For, behold, I will send serpents, cockatrices, among you, which will not be charmed, and they shall bite you, saith the LORD." Jeremiah 8:14-17*

Up to this point, the story of redemption has been a glorious thing, but now the judgment on the earth is about to fall. The seventh seal then must be what we call "The Great Tribulation." This is the time that was foretold by Christ in Matthew 24:15-22:

*"When ye therefore shall see the abomination of desolation, spoken of by Daniel the prophet, stand in the holy place, (whoso readeth, let him understand:) Then let them which be in Judaea flee into the mountains:  Let him which is on the housetop not come down to take any thing out of his house: Neither let him which is in the field return back to take his clothes. And woe unto them that are with child, and to them that give suck in those days!  But pray ye that your flight be not in the winter, neither on the sabbath day: For then shall be **great tribulation**, such as was not since the beginning of the world to this time, no, nor ever shall be. And except those days should be shortened, there should no flesh be saved: but for the elect's sake those days shall be shortened."*

The verses preceding this passage (Matthew 24:6-14) describe nation rising against nation, wars and rumors of wars, *"but the end is not yet."* That is just the *"beginning of sorrows."* Jesus then speaks of persecutions on the Jewish nation, and that they would be hated by all nations. Finally, Jesus states that the *"gospel of the kingdom"* would be preached to all nations and *"then shall the end come."* When the end comes, Jesus says they will see the *"abomination of desolation, spoken of by Daniel the prophet,"* and then He makes a peculiar statement: *"whoso readeth, let him understand."* That statement by itself identifies this is spoken to those who are reading the account not to those who are hearing it in real time. There were ten persecutions of God's people that spanned a period from 64 A.D. to 275 A.D. The hatred of God's people and the persecution of them has only continued worldwide, as the gospel of the kingdom has also spread worldwide.

This end that is to come seems to be the "Great Tribulation" which is described in graphic detail in the seventh seal.

## -Four different Accounts

Reading chapters eight through nineteen straight through as a chronological account is confusing for a couple of reasons. First, it covers only a seven-year time span. This period is divided into half and represented in several different ways:

| | |
|---|---|
| Forty and two months | Rev. 11:2 |
| 1260 days | Rev. 11:3 |
| 3 days and an half | Rev. 11:11 |
| 1260 days | Rev. 12:6 |
| A time, times, and half a time | Rev. 12:14 |
| Forty and two months | Rev. 13:5 |

Taken chronologically, adding the years together as we go, we are looking at somewhere around twenty-one years. That can't be true because Daniel's prophecy locks this period in as a week of years (7 years).

*"And he shall confirm the covenant with many for one week: and in the midst of the week he shall cause the sacrifice and the oblation to cease, and for the overspreading of abominations he shall make it desolate, even until the consummation, and that determined shall be poured upon the desolate." Daniel 9:27*

Secondly, the story comes to an end at least four different times. The first ending is in Revelation 11:15-19. This is the last of the seven trumpets. You can see a clear literary denouement in this account in verses 15 and 19:

*"And the seventh angel sounded; and there were great voices in heaven, saying, The kingdoms of this world are become the kingdoms of our Lord, and of his Christ; and he shall reign for ever and ever." Rev. 11:15*

*"And the temple of God was opened in heaven, and there was*

*seen in his temple the ark of his testament: and there were light-
nings, and voices, and thunderings, and an earthquake, and
great hail." Rev. 11:19*

The next ending is found in Revelation chapters 14 and 15. There
is quite a bit more of the ending than what I want to print here,
but these verses will direct you to the passage. Notice the visible
temple in heaven mentioned again:

*"And I saw another angel fly in the midst of heaven, having the
everlasting gospel to preach unto them that dwell on the earth,
and to every nation, and kindred, and tongue, and people, Saying with a loud voice, Fear God, and give glory to him;
for the hour of his judgment is come: and worship him that
made heaven, and earth, and the sea, and the fountains of waters. And there followed another angel, saying, Babylon is fall-
en, is fallen, that great city, because she made all nations drink
of the wine of the wrath of her fornication." Rev 14:6-8*

*"And the temple was filled with smoke from the glory of God,
and from his power; and no man was able to enter into the temple, till the seven plagues of the seven angels were fulfilled." Rev 15:8*

The third ending is found in Revelation 16:17. Notice the phrase,
"It is done":

*"And the seventh angel poured out his vial into the air; and
there came a great voice out of the temple of heaven, from the
throne, saying, It is done." Rev 16:17*

The final ending is found in Revelation chapters 18 to 20. Let's
look at two specific verses that seem to parallel what has been
recorded already:

*"And a mighty angel took up a stone like a great millstone, and
cast it into the sea, saying, Thus with violence shall that great
city Babylon be thrown down, and shall be found no more at
all." Rev 18:21*

*"And I saw heaven opened, and behold a white horse; and he that sat upon him was called Faithful and True, and in righteousness he doth judge and make war." Rev 19:11*

Each one of these accounts seems to tell the story and bring it to a close in these verses we just looked at.

There is another fact mentioned in Revelation 15:1 which seems to point to the idea that these are indeed parallel accounts. This verse references the seven angels with the seven last plagues. Arguably, we could just say that the story finally has gotten to the last seven plagues. Or… we could also take the view that there are only seven last plagues, and that these seven last plagues are represented more than once.

Following that line of thinking compare the seven trumpets to the seven vials:

**Trumpet 1**—hail and fire mingled with blood cast on the earth

> **Vial 1**– poured out vial upon the earth

**Trumpet 2**– mountain burning with fire was cast into the sea

> **Vial 2**– poured out vial upon the sea

**Trumpet 3**-wormwood falls on rivers and fountains of waters

> **Vial 3**– poured out vial on rivers and fountains of waters

**Trumpet 4**– sun, moon, and stars were smitten

> **Vial 4**– poured out vial on the sun

**Trumpet 5**-opened the bottomless pit had power to hurt men

> **Vial 5**– poured vial giving men pains and sores

**Trumpet 6**– Loose the 4 angels under the Euphrates

> **Vial 6**– poured on the river Euphrates

**Trumpet 7**– the kingdoms are become the kingdoms of our Lord

> **Vial 7**– It is done

Is it possible that the trumpets and the vials are the same last seven plagues given with a different perspective? Why would we have four different views of the same judgment? To answer those questions we must remember what the book of Revelation is about. It is about the Eternal Christ. It is about His kingship over the universe. The tribulation accounts are only important in this story as they relate to Him. Let's pause and take a look again at how the Bible presents Jesus Christ to us.

## -The Four different views of Christ

Most Bible students are familiar with the synoptic gospels: Matthew, Mark, Luke, and John. These gospels present Jesus in four different ways:

**Matthew**– Presents Christ as the King of the Jews. Matthew deals with kingdom issues and royalty. It is in this book that we get the genealogy of Christ through Abraham and David solidifying His right to the Jewish throne of David.

**Mark**– Presents Christ as the Servant of Mankind. Paul's letter to the Philippians tells us that He took upon Him the form of a servant and became obedient to death. Mark presents that interaction with humanity with the humility of the servant. It was written with the Gentile nations in mind.

**Luke**– Presents Christ as the Son of Man. In this gospel we find all of the humanity of Christ back to His Aunt Elizabeth and cousin John the Baptist. The genealogy in Luke is different than the one in Matthew because it traces the lineage of Mary back through Nathan to David.

**John**– Presents Christ as the Son of God. In this gospel written by John after he had written the book of Revelation, we see the Divinity of Christ. It begins with "In the beginning," tracing the Lord back to eternity past.

Using these examples as our guide, we can find these four same views throughout scripture.

In the Old Testament Christ is presented in four different ways in its four different divisions:

**The Books of Moses**—Show us the Kingship of the pre-incarnate Christ over Israel.

**The Books of History**– Show us His interaction with the Gentile nations through the nation of Israel.

**The Books of Poetry**– Show the humanity of the Christophany. You can see His pain in Psalms. You can see His love for His bride in the Canticles.

**The Books of Prophecy**– Once again we are presented with His absolutely Godship over His creation. He is the One and Only God of Gods and Lord of Lords.

In the New Testament divisions, we can see the same four presentations of Christ.

**The Gospels**– demonstrate His connection to Israel.

**The Acts**– demonstrates His servanthood to the world

**The Epistles**– demonstrate humanity in His Body, the Church

**The Revelation**– demonstrates the Divinity of the Eternal Christ

Compare the four parallel epistles:

**Galatians**– deals with Jewish Legalism

**Ephesians**– deals with the inclusion of the Gentiles in the Body

**Philippians**- deals with human thoughts and feelings

**Colossians**- deals with the Divinity of Christ

And then consider the Word of God as a whole. Step back and look at the four distinct presentations of Christ:

**The Old Testament–** Again we see Him as King of the Jews in all of His Glory.

**The Gospels–** Here once again we can see Him serving mankind, healing the sick, and feeding the hungry.

**The Epistles–** The Epistles are the Body of Christ in human form. We are His Body.

**The Revelation–** Again this is the pinnacle of the story. This is the Revelation of the Eternal Christ.

So then, If God introduces us to Christ in four different ways, if the tribulation accounts are intrinsically linked to the Person of the Eternal Christ, and if there are four different views of the tribulation, is it a stretch to believe that those four views might reflect the four different perspectives we are given of our Saviour?

Let's see if this holds up:

**The seven trumpets-**  this is the kingship view. The trumpets are the kings' herald. This perspective shows us His complete dominance over the Creation. It declares Him to be King of All.

**The Woman, Man-child, Beast, and False prophet–** This is the servant of mankind view. Here we see Him in the whole story connecting with all of mankind.

**The seven vials–** It's interesting to see the similarities of this view with the seven trumpets. However, we are shown the suffering of mankind here. The humanity of the tragedy shines through.

**Victory over Mystery Babylon–** This is the story that Daniel speaks of where the Stone which is cut out without hands becomes a Kingdom and infiltrates and obliterates the Mystery kingdom of Babylon.

Well, what do you think? Can you see how it fits together? Is it possible that the Lord is trying to show us four different perspectives on the last seven plagues? Following this vein let's get a little deeper into the different perspectives of the tribulation.

# -The Four Views of the Tribulation

## The First look at the Tribulation -The Seven Trumpets

The introduction to the seven trumpets is stunning. Verse one of chapter eight describes silence in heaven for about half an hour. Were they waiting for something? Were they stunned as well? It appears that this half-hour period marks a difference in the scene of heaven. There are seven angels before the throne and they are given seven trumpets. Before they begin to sound another angel comes out and stands in front of the altar of incense before the throne and he is given a golden censer which he offers along with the prayers of the saints. The Bible tells us that the smoke of the incense ascends along with the prayers of the saints up to the throne of God. These prayers would include the ones we hear the Old Testament saints praying in the fifth seal.

After the prayers have ascended the angel takes the censer and fills it with coals from off the altar and casts it to the earth. This is the apparent beginning of the Great Tribulation. The seven angels prepare themselves to play the charge and seven subsequent judgments fall on the earth.

The first four trumpets are grouped together in chapter eight. The last three trumpets are also called the three woes which the Bible indicates are worse than the first three trumpets.

*Rev. 8:13 "And I beheld, and heard an angel flying through the midst of heaven, saying with a loud voice, **Woe, woe, woe,** to the inhabiters of the earth by reason of the other voices of the trumpet of the three angels, which are yet to sound!"*

*Rev. 9:12 "**One woe** is past; and, behold, there come two woes more hereafter."*

*Rev. 11:14 "The **second woe** is past; and behold, the **third woe** cometh quickly."*

Because of the fact that the tribulation seems to be divided into two equal parts, it is possible that the first four trumpets  happen in the first half of the tribulation, and the last three trumpets, or woes, come in the last half of the tribulation.

**Trumpet 1** This trumpet pronounces judgment on the earth. Hail and fire mingled with blood is cast on the earth causing one-third of the trees and all green grass to be burnt up.

**Trumpet 2** The second trumpet sends a great mountain burning with fire into the sea and a third of the creatures in the sea die and a third part of the ships are destroyed. The burning mountain of the Old Testament comes to mind. Deuteronomy18:16 tells us about the fear of Israel in seeing the burning mountain, *"According to all that thou desiredst of the LORD thy God in Horeb in the day of the assembly, saying, Let me not hear again the voice of the LORD my God, neither let me see this great fire any more, that I die not."* There is an obvious correlation here with the judgment of God.

**Trumpet 3** The third angel brings the star called wormwood. It falls on the third part of rivers and fountains destroying a third part of the drinking water and causing many to die from it.

**Trumpet 4** The fourth trumpet smites a third part of the sun, moon, and stars causing them not to shine for a third part of the day and night.

It is interesting to see the judgment on the three parts. There is a reference to the third part of the stars being drawn by the tail of the dragon and being cast to the earth in Revelation 12:4. It seems to be talking about the angels that followed Satan. Do the third part judgments have anything to do with a third of the angels rebelling?

The final three trumpets, as we have stated, are also the final three woes. They bring us to a conclusion of the story in chapter eleven and appear to be the second half of the tribulation.

**Trumpet 5** This is the moment when the bottomless pit is open and a hoard of strange and powerful creatures are released into the earth. The bottomless pit has been alluded to before in the scriptures and this reference requires a further examination of the topic.

The very first time we are introduced to the bottomless pit is in Genesis 1:2, *"And the earth was without form, and void; and darkness was upon the face of the deep…"* The word translated "deep" in this place is the Hebrew word תהום. For those of us who don't speak Hebrew, the English transliteration of the word is "Abyss." The English definition of abyss is a bottomless chasm. Of course, at first blush, we would consider *the deep* to refer to the ocean depths which it does in part. This word is used thirty-six times in the Hebrew Old Testament, and often is referring to the ocean. The abyss then must be under the water.

This bottomless pit seems to be a prison cell of sorts. Peter makes mention of it in his second epistle (II Peter 2:4): *"For if God spared not the angels that sinned, but cast them down to hell, and delivered them into chains of darkness, to be reserved unto judgment;"* Jude also speaks of it (Jude 1:6): *"And the angels which kept not their first estate, but left their own habitation, he hath reserved in everlasting chains under darkness unto the judgment of the great day."* Satan will be bound in this same bottomless pit for 1,000 years. Jesus explains in Luke 16 that hell is in the heart of the earth, so that fact would line up with them being kept under the "deep." And I Peter 3:19 refers to it as a prison where souls are kept.

What exactly happened? When did it happen? Who is their king, "Apollyon," and what does their king do? Some of these things we will not get answers to in this life. We do know that Satan evidently fell from grace before man was created. He has already established himself as the enemy of God by Genesis 3. We also know that there are "principalities and powers in heavenly places."

There are over 800 Bible verses that mention angels and their interaction with human beings. There are "principalities and powers in heavenly places" according to Ephesians chapters three and six. What exactly their role is we don't know. There are conflicts between the heavenly bodies illustrated in Daniel's prophecy and reiterated in Revelation. The Rabbis remind us that there are some things that happen before the Torah which are sealed off from us. They teach that the beginning letter of the Torah blocks off all things before it (ב). I suppose we will have to be satisfied with what God has told us, and set aside what He hasn't told us.

The idea that water could be some sort of barrier between the spiritual world and ours is not a foreign concept in scripture. In fact, Revelation 9:14 says that four angels are bound in the great river Euphrates. So the river itself is also some kind of spiritual barrier. At the beginning of the creation God established the "bounds of our habitation" (Acts 17:26) by separating the waters from the waters and putting our known universe in the middle. *"And God said, Let there be a firmament in the midst of the waters, and let it divide the waters from the waters....And God called the firmament Heaven...And God said, Let there be lights in the firmament of the heaven to divide the day from the night...And God made two great lights; the greater light to rule the day, and lesser light to rule the night: he made the stars also."* *(See Genesis 1:6-19)* Consider also the barrier of the Red Sea, and the Jordan River which symbolizes a crossing into a new life. Peter even suggests there is something about the flood that compares to water baptism (I Peter 3:19-22). Jesus said that John's water baptism was a requirement for Himself. Was there a reason? Did the water baptism have more significance? These are all interesting questions and are worth further research in another place and time.

In summary, it appears that the watery prison was created before mankind. Judging by the name of their leader "Abaddon" or "Apollyon" which means "Destroyer," these were some pretty bad creatures. Lucifer, himself, is not even imprisoned with them.

It seems that hell, that prison in the center of the earth, is emptied at this point, and these very bad creatures are released onto the earth. They have been imprisoned for a very long time and now with their newly found freedom, they begin to destroy with a frenzy, unlike anything the world has seen before.

Because they are spiritual beings, it is quite possible that the humans whom they are attacking can not actually see them, but are the recipients of their evil designs. The descriptions are more about what they do than what can be seen.

> Scorpion stings– 5 months of physical torment
>
> Shapes of locust, teeth as lions—devouring everything
>
> Breastplates of iron—unstoppable

**Trumpet 6** The sixth angel is given the responsibility to loose the four angels which have been bound under the river Euphrates. What fascinates me is that these four angels seem to have almost the same power as the angels from the bottomless pit. They also seem to be commanders over a large army. In fact, they are probably the Destroyers that never left heaven. They are the good guys. Why are they so angry? These are most likely the same four angels that were stopped in Chapter 7. If you remember, we suggested that seal six was the crucifixion. These four angels immediately start charging the earth to destroy it, and they are told to stop until the servants of God are sealed (That's the church). Where did they go? Apparently, they are being held under the river Euphrates until this time. They will come as a revenger of God on the earth.

**Trumpet 7** This trumpet doesn't sound until the end of chapter eleven. However, chapter ten gives a kind of preface to it. In the first seven verses of chapter ten, we are introduced to another mighty angel with a  little book in his hand. He comes down from heaven and places his right foot on the sea and his left foot on the earth. He cries with a loud voice and immediately seven thunders begin to speak. What they say is a mystery because John is told to

seal up what has been said and not write it down. This is evidently the wrap-up of the tribulation because the angel declares that
time will be no longer. He also states that in the days of the voice
of the seventh angel the mystery of God will be finished.

> *"But in the days of the voice of the seventh angel, when he shall
> begin to sound, the mystery of God should be finished, as he
> hath declared to his servants the prophets." Rev. 10:7*

The rest of chapter ten sounds just like Ezekiel 3. John is given
the little book and told to eat it. With the same reaction that Ezekiel has, John finds the book to be sweet as honey in his mouth
but bitter in his belly. Ezekiel's prophecy gives us the idea that
this book contains the horrible judgments which finish off the
mystery Babylon and are apparently completely indescribable.

Chapter eleven backs up to the beginning of the seven-year tribulation and gives us a peek into something else that is going on. It
tells us what is going on with the message of Christ which is still
being preached to the world. Revelation 9:21 says that the people
enduring these horrible judgments still won't repent of their
deeds. How do they know to repent? The answer to this is explained in Rev. 11:1-4.

Power is given to God's two witnesses for 1260 days (3.5 years)
to prophesy. These two witnesses are the two olive trees and the
two candlesticks which stand before the God of the earth. Who
are they? Zechariah speaks of them in his prophecy:

> *"And said unto me, What seest thou? And I said, I have looked,
> and behold a candlestick all of gold, with a bowl upon the top of
> it, and his seven lamps thereon, and seven pipes to the seven
> lamps, which are upon the top thereof: And two olive trees by it,
> one upon the right side of the bowl, and the other upon the left
> side thereof. So I answered and spake to the angel that talked
> with me, saying, What are these, my lord? Then the angel that
> talked with me answered and said unto me, Knowest thou not
> what these be? And I said, No, my lord. Then he answered and*

*spake unto me, saying, This is the word of the LORD unto Zerubbabel, saying, Not by might, nor by power, but by my spirit, saith the LORD of hosts......Then answered I, and said unto him, What are these two olive trees upon the right side of the candlestick and upon the left side thereof? And I answered again, and said unto him, What be these two olive branches which through the two golden pipes empty the golden oil out of themselves? And he answered me and said, Knowest thou not what these be? And I said, No, my lord. Then said he, These are the two anointed ones, that stand by the Lord of the whole earth." Zechariah 4:2-14*

If we use Matthew 17 and the mount of transfiguration as a guide, as well as the activities that these two are engaged in (Rev. 11:5-6), we would quickly conclude that these two olive trees must be Moses and Elijah. However, there may be more to it than that. Maybe Moses and Elijah represent a larger group.

It appears that these witnesses preach for the first half of the tribulation and then are killed. It looks like their dead bodies are left to rot in the open for three and a half days. The three and a half days may be a prophetical reference to the last three and a half years of the tribulation. At the end of that time period they are raptured in the same way as the church (I Thessalonians 4/ Revelation 4) - resurrected and then gathered together with us in the cloud. There are prophecies in the Old Testament of this time when the two witnesses will be lying in the streets. Asaph writes about it in a psalm:

*"O God, the heathen are come into thine inheritance; thy holy temple have they defiled; they have laid Jerusalem on heaps. The dead bodies of thy servants have they given to be meat unto the fowls of the heaven, the flesh of thy saints unto the beasts of the earth. Their blood have they shed like water round about Jerusalem; and there was none to bury them." Psalm 79:1-3*

Jeremiah speaks of this time as well:

> *"At that time, saith the LORD, they shall bring out the bones of the kings of Judah, and the bones of his princes, and the bones of the priests, and the bones of the prophets, and the bones of the inhabitants of Jerusalem, out of their graves: And they shall spread them before the sun, and the moon, and all the host of heaven, whom they have loved, and whom they have served, and after whom they have walked, and whom they have sought, and whom they have worshipped: they shall not be gathered, nor be buried; they shall be for dung upon the face of the earth. And death shall be chosen rather than life by all the residue of them that remain of this evil family, which remain in all the places whither I have driven them, saith the LORD of hosts." Jeremiah 8:1-3*

If these Old Testament references are speaking of the same events as Revelation eleven, then we must assume more than two people are witnessing, being killed, and left in the streets. Is this possible? Who could these two groups of people be?

Zechariah's prophecy indicates that they are connected to the Word of the Lord. So they are obviously believers. Is it possible that we are referring to Israel as the nation and possibly a remnant of the church? I do believe that the church, as we know it, will be raptured before the tribulation begins. However, for the first three and a half years of the tribulation, there will still be a remnant of writings and messages left by the church. Gentiles who reject the Anti-Christ message will be drawn to this message. Some will choose not to take the mark of the beast (Rev. 15:2).

Consider the twenty-four elders. These elders are mentioned six times throughout the book of Revelation and seem to be representatives of believers: Revelation 4:4, 4:10, 5:3, 5:14, 11:16, 19:4.

Revelation twenty-one speaks of two groups of twelve in the New Jerusalem: the twelve tribes of Israel and the twelve apostles.

Revelation twelve speaks of two groups that are the remnant of the seed of the woman: those "which keep the commandments of God" and those who "have the testimony of Jesus Christ." Revelation fifteen speaks of those who "sing the song of Moses" and those who "sing the song of the Lamb." Revelation twenty speaks of those who were beheaded for "The witness of Jesus," and "for the word of God." In each one of these instances, one can see how two different groups of witnesses are possibly being identified. Could it be that Israel will still be present representing God and also believers in Jesus will be present representing our Lord?

When all of those who refuse the mark and resist the falling away of God's creation are killed, then those who have "chosen" death (Jer.8:3) will rejoice. Is it possible that the middle of the tribulation will be marked by the killing of all those who still have chosen to believe in Jesus? And that Israel, the chosen nation, will be sent into hiding? Is it possible that for the next three and a half years there will be no "water of the word?" Will this be the time prophesied by Amos:

*"Behold, the days come, saith the Lord GOD, that I will send a famine in the land, not a famine of bread, nor a thirst for water, but of hearing the words of the LORD:" Amos 8:11*

 Maybe the three and a half years of drought during Elijah's time was a prophetic picture of the last three and half years of the tribulation (James 5:17). This is definitely a viable theory.

When these martyred witnesses are resurrected and raptured to join us, an earthquake will destroy one-tenth of the city of Jerusalem and will kill 7,000 people.

And then… The seventh angel will sound his trumpet. The kingdoms of the world will become the Kingdoms of our Lord and of his Christ at this time. The temple of God will be opened and the King will take what is His. This will bring the tribulation to a close. There are three more perspectives given of the tribulation and triumphal entry of Christ yet to come.

**The Second look at the Tribulation**

This view spans Revelation 12-14. It is a quick overview in the same vein as Mark's gospel. We see Christ as the servant of mankind, offering himself to the world.

First comes the story of the woman (Israel) who gives birth to the man child (Jesus Christ). The dragon (Satan) appears attempting to destroy the man child as soon as he is born. The woman gives birth and her child is caught up to God and to His throne (Acts 1). Then the woman flees to the wilderness and is hidden away for 1260 days (three and a half years). This must be the second half of the tribulation. The dragon is kicked out of heaven and cast to the earth along with his angels. This is the same time that the bottomless pit would be opened. During that last half of the tribulation, the dragon will persecute the woman (Israel) and try to destroy her. This is the time when all believers will go into hiding or be killed (Rev. 12:17).

Next, we see how the Beast rises to power. Revelation 13:5-7 tells us that he is given the power to overcome the saints for forty -two months (3 and a half years). He begins to blaspheme God and sets himself up as God (II Thessalonians 2:4). This is the abomination of desolations spoken of by Daniel the prophet (Daniel 9:27) and this is the moment when Jesus tells the Jews to flee (Matt. 24:15).

The second beast arrives on the scene. This one is also called the false prophet (Rev.13:11-18, 19:20). He is the one who establishes the worship of the Beast. He sets up a program that forces everyone to receive a mark in their right hand or in their foreheads. Only those with this mark can buy or sell in this new economy.

We are well acquainted with the number 666, which is the number of the beast. Revelation 13:18 says, *"Here is wisdom. Let him that hath understanding count the number of the beast: for it is the number of a man; and his number is six hundred three score and six."* We can easily get confused on this topic. So let's be careful to just try to understand it from what the Bible tells us about this number.

Fact #1 *"Here is wisdom."* This statement immediately connects to the book of Proverbs. *"The fear of the LORD is the beginning of wisdom: and the knowledge of the holy is understanding." Proverbs 9:10* Because the fear of the Lord is where wisdom begins, it seems possible that this is a very important part of the warning. Jesus reminds us to not fear the one who only has power over the body, but to fear the One who can cast both body and soul into eternal fire (Matthew 10:28). Maybe this is a reminder to those believers who are given the option of taking the mark or dying that death is far preferable to eternal damnation. On a side note, Proverbs was compiled by King Solomon, who happens to be the only other one in the Bible connected to this number (I Kings 10:14).

Fact #2 *"Let him that hath understanding."* This is directed to a specific group of people. Most of us would like to believe that we are those who have an understanding of the times. However, this may be speaking to those who are actually looking at the choice in front of them. This might be a direct address to those believers in the tribulation who are facing annihilation.  Here is an interesting prophecy about this exact time by the prophet Daniel:

*"And arms shall stand on his part, and they shall pollute the sanctuary of strength, and shall take away the daily sacrifice, and they shall place the abomination that maketh desolate. And such as do wickedly against the covenant shall he corrupt by flatteries: but the people that do know their God shall be strong, and do exploits. And they that understand among the people shall instruct many: yet they shall fall by the sword, and by flame, by captivity, and by spoil, many days.... but many shall cleave to them with flatteries. And some of them of understanding shall fall, to try them, and to purge, and to make them white, even to the time of the end: because it is yet for a time appointed." Daniel 11:31-35*

Fact#3 *"Count the number of the beast."* Counting the number is interesting. I have collected a few interesting mathematical anomalies involving this number for your perusal. I am not certain what all of these facts mean, but they are fascinating.

- In Roman numerals 600 is DC, 60 is LX, and 6 is VI. Thus DCLXVI is 666 and uses all the Roman numeral characters less than M (1000) exactly one time.

- $2^2 + 3^2 + 5^2 + 7^2 + 11^2 + 13^2 + 17^2 = 666$; the numbers being squared are the first seven prime numbers.

- $6^2 \times 6^2 - 6^2 = 1260$ (half of the tribulation)

- 666 is the sum total of the first 36 (6x6) numbers

- 666 is the largest repdigit triangular number. It is also a palindrome.

- The exponents in the prime factorization are 1, 2, and 1. Adding one to each and multiplying we get $(1 + 1)(2 + 1)(1 + 1) = 2 \times 3 \times 2 = 12$. Therefore 666 has exactly 12 factors.

- Factors of 666: 1, 2, 3, 6, 9, 18, 37, 74, 111, 222, 333, 666

Fact #4 *"For it is the number of a man"* Six is the number of man. The number of man being listed three times could be a clear statement that the trichotomy (Body, soul, and spirit) of the beast is purely human. Some have tried to say that he will be half angel/half man. This number would suggest otherwise. Is it possible that God is telling the believers at that time to not be afraid of man? This beast literally can not do any more than he is allowed to do. He is not God, he is all man. This reminds us of the first fact—the fear of God is the beginning of wisdom. We should not fear what man can do to us (Hebrews 13:6).

Fact#5 *"And his number is Six hundred three score and six."* John did not spell out the numbers that we see in the English translation, he penned it as the Greek word Χξς. This steers us toward the idea of gematria. Gematria is the study that was developed to calculate the numerical value of letters and words. We get our word geometry from this word. Each letter of the Hebrew alphabet has a numerical significance. The Greek alphabet also has numerical significance. Be careful with this because "Figures don't lie, but liars figure." you can manipulate these numbers to get names of presidents and politicians which really have no significance at all to the truth in this verse. However, a study of numbers and number codes in the Bible will leave you

The rest of the story in this account of the tribulation continues into chapter fourteen. Here once again we are introduced to the 144,000 which we covered in some detail in the previous chapter. In this case, they are following the Lamb. They appear to be heading toward earth. This would be the same moment reflected in Revelation 19:14: *"The armies which were in heaven followed him upon white horses, clothed in fine linen, white and clean."*

Just before this section records the ending fall of Babylon we find another interesting part of the story not mentioned before. Read it first and then comments will follow:

*"And I saw another angel fly in the midst of heaven, having the everlasting gospel to preach unto them that dwell on the earth, and to every nation, and kindred, and tongue, and people, Saying with a loud voice, Fear God, and give glory to him; for the hour of his judgment is come: and worship him that made heaven, and earth, and the sea, and the fountains of waters." Revelation 14:6-7*

I find it interesting that we have come to the end of a three-and-a-half-year period with no Bible message of any kind. All religion has changed to worship the beast and therefore in just that short time, no one remembers Jesus or the cross. The message to the world, in summary is, "Worship the Creator." Everyone is without excuse according to Romans chapter one. All of us are born with this God-consciousness, knowing that judgment is coming. According to this prophecy, many people will refuse to worship the beast and will be killed because of it. However, in some places, there will be pockets of people. You might call them "the corners of the field," and this angel is gleaning those corners. There is no mention of the Lamb at this point because truly they have no idea of Who He is. God's grace and mercy is still preparing a place for them if they will but respond to what they are able to understand.

The Final part of this section (Revelation 14:8-20) describes the fall of Babylon, which we see in greater detail in chapters seventeen to nineteen. The added story of the angel thrusting his sickle into the earth and reaping is also described in Joel 3:9-16. This is the place where we find out that blood will be up to the horses' bridles at the end of the horrific battle of Armageddon.

**The Third look at the tribulation—the seven vials**

This third look is covered in chapter fifteen and sixteen. Remember the parallel to the third perspective of Christ. Luke's gospel presents Him as the Son of Man showing his human connection and suffering. So in this view we see the human suffering which comes from each of the seven trumpets.

We start in chapter fifteen with the view from heaven. The scene plays out almost as a replay for those who have been victorious during the tribulation. (Don't forget, this entire scene is being played out in God's time-line which is not the same as ours.) We find those tribulation saints present during this time. They stand with us on the same sea of glass which we found in chapter four. They are singing the song of Moses and the song of the Lamb. The temple in heaven is opened and the vials full of the wrath of God is given to the seven angels. The temple is filled with smoke from the glory of God and no one can enter the temple until the plagues are fulfilled. The dedication of Solomon's temple had a shadow portrayal of this moment (II Chron. 7:1-2).

Now, instead of trumpets sounding the charge, vials are poured out on the earth. If you go back and look at the seven trumpets, you will see distinct parallels.

**Vial 1** It is poured out on the earth, and the result produces a horrible sore on those who worship the Beast.

**Vial 2** It is poured out on the sea, and the result is that the sea becomes blood killing every living soul in the sea. Compare this to the second trumpet when a third of ships and a third of the living creatures die. What's different here is the focus on the people. All of those who are on the ships in the sea, every living soul dies.

**Vial 3** It is poured out on the rivers and fountains of water, and the result is all of the drinking water becomes blood. Again the focus is on what humans have to drink.

**Vial 4** This vial is poured out on the sun, the result being that men are scorched with great heat. The fourth trumpet also speaks of judgment on the sun, but it talks of the darkness that covers the earth for a third of the day and a third of the night. The vial explains that the curse on the sun also produces a great heat resulting in world-wide sunburning on the people.

**Vial 5** This speaks of the seat of the beast who has set himself up as god in the middle of the tribulation. Here are described pains and sores that can not be healed. They are literally gnawing their tongues because of the pain. The Fifth trumpet describes the unleashing of the hoards from the bottomless pit with stings like scorpions. We see in this view the results of their work.

**Vial 6** At this time we see the reference to the great river Euphrates just like the sixth trumpet. The water is dried up releasing the angels which were bound underneath it (described with the sounding of the sixth trumpet). Following this vial we see that the dragon, the beast, and the false prophet work miracles and deceive people to follow them to Armageddon. This is also described in the second view of the tribulation in greater detail (Rev. 13:12-15).

**Vial 7** The seventh vial brings us once again to the destruction of

Babylon. In this account, we find that one-third of Babylon falls. We know this is speaking of Mystery Babylon because it uses the identifier: "the great city."

> *"And there followed another angel, saying, Babylon is fallen, is fallen, that great city, because she made all nations drink of the wine of the wrath of her fornication." Rev.14:8*

> *"Standing afar off for the fear of her torment, saying, Alas, alas, that great city Babylon, that mighty city! for in one hour is thy judgment come." Rev.18:10*

> *"And a mighty angel took up a stone like a great millstone, and cast it into the sea, saying, Thus with violence shall that great city Babylon be thrown down, and shall be found no more at all." Rev.18:21*

Notice that just before the sounding of the seventh trumpet one-tenth of the city is destroyed. The tenth speaks of a tithe which is the covenant with Israel, leading me to believe it is referring to Jerusalem (Rev. 11:13).

The events that transpire here look a little bit like the six seal which describes the events around the crucifixion. Compare the two and you will see that the Substitutionary Sacrifice has been taken away at the second event. In chapter six they pray for the rocks to fall on them and hide them from the One on the throne and from the Lamb. In chapter sixteen they actually have hail stones (those rocks they prayed for), but there is no mention of the King on the throne or of the Lamb. Instead, they begin to blaspheme God.

> *"A great earthquake.." Rev. 6:12*

> *"A great earthquake, such as was not since men were upon the earth, so mighty an earthquake, and so great." Rev. 16:18*

> *"...And every mountain and island were moved out of their places." Rev. 6:14*

*"And every island fled away, and mountains were not found."*
*Rev. 16:20*

*"And said to the mountains and rocks, Fall on us, and hide us
from the face of him that sitteth on the throne, and from the
wrath of the Lamb." Rev. 6:16*

*"And there fell upon men a great hail out of heaven, every stone
about the weight of a talent: and men blasphemed God because
of the plague of the hail; for the plague thereof was exceeding
great." Rev. 16:21*

## The Fourth look at the tribulation—Divine Judgment

As we have mentioned before this perspective coincides with the
same view we get of Jesus in John's Gospel. John begins his gospel with the words, *"In the beginning was the Word, and the
Word was with God and the Word was God."* In the same manner, this explanation jumps right to the total destruction of the
tower of Babel and the effort that humankind has made to build a
name in God's universe without God.

Mystery Babylon is the kingdom effort that began in Genesis
eleven with the tower of Babel. It is man's effort to govern himself without God. The description of her destruction is very
graphic, but there are some key elements we need to take note of
to direct our understanding.

**Mystery Babylon** This city is described in great detail by the
prophet Daniel (Daniel 2:31-45) while he explained the dream of
Nebuchadnezzar. A common mistake made by Bible students is
to assume that the kingdoms of the Old Testament were primitive
and very localized. When we say "world-wide" in the Old Testament we forget that indeed the entire world was "overspread" by
the descendants of Noah (Genesis 19:19). Researching these kingdoms you will find that indeed their reach extended way beyond
Mesopotamia. One of the Persian kings claimed to have sent
thousands of explorers into all the corners of the globe collecting
anything of interest to be brought back for study. Consider how a

handful of explorers changed the lives of Europeans, and then consider the reign of an absolute monarch with unlimited resources.

The image Daniel describes is a human form. The head of the image is pure gold and Nebuchadnezzar's kingdom is said to be this head of gold. His kingdom encompassed the entire world.

The shoulders and arms are silver and history soon indicates that this is the great Media-Persia empire.

The belly and thighs of brass represent the Grecian empire that followed. Just before the time of Christ, the trade language of the world was Greek.

The legs of iron come next on the image, which seems to be the Roman empire divided into its two parts.

Following the Roman empire is this strange kingdom which is described as two feet with 10 specific toes (more on the toes later) and is part iron and part clay. The remnants of the Roman empire are still there, but it has this clay mixed in which makes the iron weak. Daniel describes it this way:

*"...They shall mingle themselves with the seed of men: but they shall not cleave one to another, even as iron is not mixed with clay." Daniel 2:43*

This kingdom looks a lot like the kingdoms of our times. Latin (the Roman trade language) is the basis for our English language, as well as, every other European language. Our Calendar is part Roman. July is named for Julius Caesar. August is named for Augustus Caesar. The Roman gods adorn the weekdays of the romance languages. In Spanish the days of the week are lunes, martes, miercoles, jueves, viernes. In French they are lundi, mardi, mercredi, jeudi, and vendredi. It isn't hard to see the Roman gods, *Luna, Mars, Mercurius, Iovis* and *Venus* in those names. Our system of government is a hybrid with parts coming from different ideas of thought. The Senate and its oratorical practices come right out of Roman politics. The racial tension that we see in almost every country lines up with Daniel's prophecy that the mingled seed will not "cleave one to another."

When we read chapter eighteen about the complete devastation of Mystery Babylon and how this devastation has a dynamic effect on the commerce of the entire world, our first instinct is to relate it to what we know. As an American, I can see the American dollar and the American democracy and capitalistic system affecting the whole of the world. If you are reading this, and you are from China you might think that the Chinese exports are being referred to. If you are from the European Union, you might see the Euro or the European school of thought as the basis for this. One might even note the United Nations and all of its global impact. All of these perspectives could be correct.

The story of Mystery Babylon begins in Genesis 11 with the tower of Babel. This is the place that birthed the idea that man could govern himself without God. It was there that God reminded man that he was a created being and answerable to a Higher Power. The idea of governing without God and seizing supreme power for human use grew into this giant creature which the Bible calls "Mystery, Babylon the Great, the Mother of Harlots and Abominations of the Earth." This mystical creature took on a life of its own reaching its tentacles into every corner of human governance. Even Christians in our day get faint-hearted when thinking that their way of life might be disrupted. Materialism is the driving force. Capitalism in all of it's glory is the vehicle which she exploits.

Remember fornication and adultery is the shadow of a deeper problem, that is, worshipping the creature more than the Creator (Rom. 1:25). Fornication represents idolatry in the scriptures in the same way that leprosy represents sin. So calling Mystery Babylon by the name, "The great whore," (Rev. 17:1) points us to the idea that Babylon is about worshipping and serving man as a god.

The story is very specific about the ten horns which align themselves with the Beast. It seems to be the same as the ten toes of Daniel's image and will be the last kingdoms to raise themselves against God. They, however, do not strengthen the kingdom of Babylon. Instead, they are used by God to destroy it.

> *"And the ten horns which thou sawest are ten kings, which have received no kingdom as yet; but receive power as kings one hour with the beast. These have one mind, and shall give their power and strength unto the beast." Rev. 17:11-12*

The verse above seems to indicate that these kingdoms do not currently exist, but will grow out of the policies of the Anti-Christ ruler. There will be ten of them and they will be completely united in spirit with him. They will hate Babylon even though they have grown out of her and will end up completely destroying her.

> *"And the ten horns which thou sawest upon the beast, these shall hate the whore, and shall make her desolate and naked, and shall eat her flesh, and burn her with fire. For God hath put in their hearts to fulfill his will, and to agree, and give their kingdom unto the beast, until the words of God shall be fulfilled." Rev. 17:16-17*

We can see in Daniel's prophecy (Daniel 2:34-35) that the end of the Mystery Babylon Kingdom will come when the Stone cut out without hands crushes the feet of the image. This is the moment when the King of kings rides into view with the armies of the saints behind Him.

This last view of the Tribulation ends with our focus returning to the scene in heaven. Once again we see the "four and twenty elders" and the four beasts from around the throne. Then we hear the sound of a great multitude like the sound of a crashing sea or a powerful thunderstorm saying, *"Alleluia: for the Lord God Omnipotent reigneth."*

# Section 4

**Chapter:** Eight

**Title:** The Throne of David

**Summary:** This is the period we call the Millennium. It is the thousand-year reign of Christ on earth. It is the Kingdom of Christ in full display. It appears to be the Marriage supper leading up to the wedding. All of the saints will be serving at this time in different capacities.

**Study Outline:**

1.  David's everlasting throne
2.  Saint's reigning with Christ
3.  Satan's ultimate defeat
4.  The Great White Throne

# The Throne of David

Immediately following this declaration that "The Lord God omnipotent reigneth," our attention is turned to the Bride (Rev. 19:7-9). The marriage ceremony of the Lamb is getting ready to begin. The Bride has on her white wedding garments. They are specifically described as "the righteousness of saints." At this point, righteousness has been granted. All of the saints have been declared justified because of the masterful argument of our Lawyer, our "Advocate with the Father, Jesus Christ the righteous" (I John 2:2). It is now time for Him to claim His throne.

Heaven is opened for the fourth time in the book of Revelation. The first time was when John was raptured (4:1), The second and third times are referring to the final judgment time (11:19, 15:5). There are Five other times heaven is described as being open in the scriptures. I will list them here as an additional contextual study:

1. Genesis 7:11 The flood

2. Malachi 3:10  Blessings from heaven

3. Luke 3:21 The Spirit descending on Jesus

4. John 1:51 Prophecy of the Glory of Jesus

5. Acts 10:11 Gentiles to be included in the church

## David's everlasting Throne

The Throne of David was established by God as an everlasting throne. The prophecies of the Old Testament do not seem to match the history that followed...Until we get to this point in time. Let's go back and look at some of those prophecies to get a sense of what this Millennial reign is.

*"And king Solomon shall be blessed, and the throne of David shall be established before the LORD for ever." 1Kings 2:45*

*" Then I will establish the throne of thy kingdom upon Israel for ever, as I promised to David thy father, saying, There shall not fail thee a man upon the throne of Israel." I Kings 9:5*

*"The LORD hath sworn in truth unto David; he will not turn from it; Of the fruit of thy body will I set upon thy throne." Psalm 132:11*

*"Of the increase of his government and peace there shall be no end, upon the throne of David, and upon his kingdom, to order it, and to establish it with judgment and with justice from henceforth even for ever. The zeal of the LORD of hosts will perform this." Isaiah 9:7*

*" For thus saith the LORD; David shall never want a man to sit upon the throne of the house of Israel;" Jeremiah 33:17*

*"He shall be great, and shall be called the Son of the Highest: and the Lord God shall give unto him the throne of his father David:" Luke 1:32*

There was a very specific promise that God would put a King on the throne of David forever. The problem came when Israel and her kings began to worship idols and drifted clear away from God. It got so bad that God placed a curse on the line of David to the point that no one would ever be able to fill the throne again.

*"Therefore thus saith the LORD of Jehoiakim king of Judah; He shall have none to sit upon the throne of David: and his dead*

*body shall be cast out in the day to the heat, and in the night to the frost." Jeremiah 36:30*

Joseph, the carpenter stepfather of Jesus, was actually in the direct line of the kings of Israel. He had the legal right to the throne and, had it not been for the apostasy and falling away of Israel, would have been the king of Israel. The genealogy of Matthew proves his right to the throne. Jesus, his firstborn, obtained the birthright of the Davidic throne through Joseph but did not receive the curse because He was not in the bloodline of Joseph. Luke's genealogy shows us that Jesus was still descended from David through Mary. The difference in the genealogies is striking. Joseph descends from David through Solomon. Mary descends through David's second son of Bathsheba, Nathan, who is ironically named after the prophet who called out David's sin.

Jesus has not yet claimed this throne. He was crucified during His first visit to the earth. However, at His second coming, He will completely fulfill the prophecies concerning the everlasting throne of David. Consider the following verses:

*"And in the days of these kings shall the God of heaven set up a kingdom, which shall never be destroyed: and the kingdom shall not be left to other people, but it shall break in pieces and consume all these kingdoms, and it shall stand for ever." Daniel 2:44*

*"And saviours shall come up on mount Zion to judge the mount of Esau; and the kingdom shall be the LORD'S." Obadiah 1:21*

*"When the Son of man shall come in his glory, and all the holy angels with him, then shall he sit upon the throne of his glory:" Matthew 25:31*

When Jesus began His earthly ministry, He started by saying, "The kingdom of heaven is at hand." Throughout the book of Matthew and even on into the other gospels, He would teach by parables about this "kingdom of heaven." If you put all of the prophecies and comments together about the kingdom, it appears that it comes in four phases.

The first phase of the kingdom is the construction phase spoken of by Daniel (2:44):

*"And in the days of these kings shall the God of heaven set up a kingdom, which shall never be destroyed: and the kingdom shall not be left to other people, but it shall break in pieces and consume all these kingdoms, and it shall stand for ever."*

Notice how it speaks of the creation of the kingdom during the days of the kings of Mystery Babylon. It began with Israel rebuilding the temple and making a place for the Messiah to come. John the Baptist would have been part of this phase.

The second phase begins at Pentecost. We call it the church. Some might even say the Universal Church. It is without question a mystery kingdom as explained in all of the kingdom parables.

The third phase of the kingdom would be during the thousand-year reign of Christ on earth. This is the period we are dealing with in this chapter. The prophecies of the everlasting throne could not possibly mean this time because it has a very definite ending. Yet, it is still part of the Kingdom of Christ.

The fourth phase would be the eternal throne which would last beyond the end of the world and would be set up in the new heaven and earth. This would be the time we are one with Christ as He prayed in John 17.

Sometimes you will find the kingdom referenced as a mystery body, and sometimes you will find it described as an actual kingdom on earth. Understanding which part is being referenced is critical to understanding the message.

We finally have arrived at this point in the book of Revelation where Jesus returns with his saints to set up His kingdom. This is a physical, visible return and will mark the end of the tribulation period. What a glorious scene is described!

Heaven is opened and a white horse comes out of heaven. This is the same white horse as found in the first seal. However, this time it is ridden by the second Adam, Jesus Christ.

The crowns on His head are possibly the ones given to Him in Revelation 4:10 by the 24 elders who represent the believers of all time. The name written which only He knows indicates there are still mysteries that are His alone. His clothes are dipped in Blood, and He is called the Word of God.

All of the armies following Him are the saints mentioned in Revelation 19:7-8. Everyone who has put their trust in Him from the Garden to the Coming will be in that army. You will see once again in Revelation 19:14 that a specific reference is made to their riding also on white horses. This seems to be a direct reference to the white horse of Revelation 6. The saints are restored to their proper place on the white horse with the authority and power in their hands. This is the same scene predicted by Enoch, the seventh from Adam (Jude 1:14-15). Paul makes mention of our meeting Him in the clouds before this return (I Thess. 4:17). Deuteronomy 33:2 and  Psalm 50:5 are also verses of interest to this subject.

Jesus, Himself, is coming to rule as KING OF KINGS AND LORD OF LORDS. The sword proceeding out of His mouth kills all resistance. The last verse of chapter 14 tells us that blood is up to the horses' bridles. The birds are called to clean up the mess, and it is called "The supper of the great God."

The Beast and the False prophet are both taken and cast alive into the Lake of Fire. They are the first ones to occupy this eternal damnation. There is no throne judgment. They are simply cast directly into the judgment. Satan is bound at this time and cast into the bottomless pit which has recently been emptied of all of the fallen angels (Rev. 9:2) which have been held there since before the earth was (II Peter 2:4, Jude 1:6).

It at this time that Jesus claims the throne of David.

## Saints reigning with Christ

The truth that the saints would reign with the Lord in His glory is something so part of the fabric of Jewish thought that they sang about it. Psalms 149 is one such song. Read this Psalm and notice phrases like: "...a new song..." and "a two-edged sword in their hand. And then the last verse says that the execution of judgment on the heathen is an honor given to all saints:

*Praise ye the LORD. Sing unto the LORD a new song, and his praise in the congregation of saints.*

*Let Israel rejoice in him that made him: let the children of Zion be joyful in their King.*

*Let them praise his name in the dance: let them sing praises unto him with the timbrel and harp.*

*For the LORD taketh pleasure in his people: he will beautify the meek with salvation.*

*Let the saints be joyful in glory: let them sing aloud upon their beds.*

*Let the high praises of God be in their mouth, and a twoedged sword in their hand;*

*To execute vengeance upon the heathen, and punishments upon the people;*

*To bind their kings with chains, and their nobles with fetters of iron;*

*To execute upon them the judgment written: this honour have all his saints. Praise ye the LORD.*

The following list of verses also reflects the idea that the saints will one day rule over the earth:

*"But the saints of the most High shall take the kingdom, and possess the kingdom for ever, even for ever and ever." Daniel 7:18*

*"Until the Ancient of days came, and judgment was given to the saints of the most High; and the time came that the saints possessed the kingdom." Daniel 7:22*

*"Do ye not know that the saints shall judge the world? and if the world shall be judged by you, are ye unworthy to judge the smallest matters?" I Corinthians 6:2*

*"And Enoch also, the seventh from Adam, prophesied of these, saying, Behold, the Lord cometh with ten thousands of his saints," Jude 1:14*

The disciples were very much interested in this idea and asked the Lord questions concerning their place in the kingdom. Most notably the mother of James and John requested that they be given a place of honor in His kingdom. Matthew records (chapter 24) a time when the disciples came to Jesus asking Him when He was coming back, and when the end of the world was. Luke tells the story in Acts 1:7-11 of Jesus giving His disciples instructions before He left. Their question to Him was, *"...Lord, wilt thou at this time restore again the kingdom to Israel?"* This was a topic of great interest to them, and they received their answer after Jesus ascended into heaven in front of them. The angel said to them, *"...this same Jesus, which is taken up from you into heaven, shall so come in like manner as ye have seen him go into heaven."* Why is He coming back? To establish His kingdom on earth.

Jesus spoke of the saints ruling in this earthly kingdom four different times in the days leading up to his crucifixion.

- Matthew 24:42-51 He speaks of the faithful and wise servant who is ruler over His household. When He comes and finds that servant faithfully taking care of the household He will reward him by making him ruler over all of His goods.

- Matthew 25:1-13 The wise and foolish are separated here by the oil which they had. The wise had enough oil to spare right up to the coming of the Lord. However, the foolish ran out of oil. When they realized they did not have enough they went to buy more oil and did not make it back in time for the feast. Some have suggested that the foolish virgins are actually the Jews who continue to worship Jehovah but miss the point of the sacrifice of Jesus.

- Matthew 25:14-30 This is the story of the talents. Three different servants are given talents according to their abilities. The first two used their talents and were able to increase them. Their reward was that the Lord would make them ruler over many things, and they were instructed to enter into the joy of the Lord. The third servant did nothing with his gift and was punished for it.

- Matthew 25:31-46 The righteous were identified in this story as those who had clothed the naked and visited the sick and those in prison, etc. They were told that they would inherit the "kingdom prepared for you from the foundation of the world."

In each one of these stories Jesus states that there is a kingdom coming to earth where rewards will be given and rewards will be taken. He is specific about the fact that saints will rule and reign with Him.

All of these verses seem to be pointing to this time mentioned in Revelation 20:4:

*"And I saw thrones, and they sat upon them, and judgment was given unto them: and I saw the souls of them that were beheaded for the witness of Jesus, and for the word of God, and which had not worshipped the beast, neither his image, neither had received his mark upon their foreheads, or in their hands; and they lived and reigned with Christ a thousand years."*

It is during this time that the original authority given to mankind in the first seal (Rev. 6) will be realized. The Bible indicates that authority is given to the saints based on their faithfulness in this life. The ruling is done with a rod of iron, and open sin will not be tolerated. How it will all work exactly is still a mystery, but Jesus,

Himself will be on the Throne of David in person in Jerusalem.

## Satan's Ultimate Defeat

*"And I saw an angel come down from heaven, having the key of the bottomless pit and a great chain in his hand. And he laid hold on the dragon, that old serpent, which is the Devil, and Satan, and bound him a thousand years," Revelation 20:1-2*

Satan's reign of terror started before the world began. Long before time as we know it existed, Satan was created to be in God's presence and serve Him. Isaiah 14 refers to him as "Lucifer," which means "Light bearer" indicating his function with the giving of light. Ezekiel 28 also seems to be a reference to Satan before his fall. While the specific prophecy begins with a pronouncement against the King of Tyre, it quickly turns and seems to be projecting on Satan, himself.

Sometime in the pre-world era, an insurrection took place. We draw this conclusion because of the reference to the fallen angels who are kept in chains being held until the end time (II Peter 2:4). There is also a reference to a holding place called "the bottomless pit" (Revelation 9:1-12), which had a king over them called, "Abaddon" in Hebrew, and "Apollyon" in Greek. Both names mean "Destroyer." Who is this king and what exactly is his role? I have no idea. In fact, we are cautioned in Colossians 2:18-19 not to worship angels putting them on a pedestal that is not for them, and we are commanded not to intrude into things that we have not seen.

By the time Adam and Eve are in the Garden of Eden, Satan has already established himself as the opponent of God and His will. There is no exact record of when Satan established himself in this way. However, in Genesis 1:2 the word "deep" is translated from the Hebrew word "abyss" (English transliteration), which is the name ascribed to the bottomless pit by the Jewish people. This fact, along with the direct statement that God separated the light from the darkness in the fourth verse of the first chapter of the

Bible, directs me to the conclusion that Satan's iniquity began before the world was formed to be inhabited by man. Ephesians chapter three adds to this idea by stating that the plan of Salvation was in the mind of God from the beginning of the world and that the eternal purpose of the church is to help the principalities and powers in heavenly places know the manifold wisdom of God.

> *"And to make all men see what is fellowship of the mystery, which from the beginning of the world hath been hid in God, who created all things by Jesus Christ: To the intent that now unto the principalities and powers in heavenly places might be known by the church the manifold wisdom of God, according to the eternal purpose which he purposed in Christ Jesus our Lord:" Ephesians 3:9-11*

Throughout the ages, we are given little glimpses of the conflicts in Heaven between Satan and the Angels who remained faithful to God.

One Old Testament book tells us of the challenge God made to Satan concerning the man from Uz whose name was Job. The book of Daniel explains to us that the angel Gabriel was hindered by a heavenly prince in his mission to bring the prophet Daniel a message. The story is recorded that Gabriel had to call on reinforcements from the angel Michael so that he could get to the prophet. In the book of Jude we find that Michael and Satan argued over the body of Moses. Satan wanted the body of Moses for his own purposes.

It is not until Revelation twelve that we find complete victory by the hosts of heaven over Satan. This victory is described in Revelation 12:7-12. The deciding factors in this historic win are "The blood of Jesus" and "the word of their testimony" (testimony of the saints). We are the deciding factor.

When heaven is opened and the King of Kings leads us out of heaven back to the earth to set up his throne, the beast (the Anti-Christ) and the false prophet are immediately captured and cast alive into the Eternal Lake of Fire. Then an angel comes down from heaven with a great chain and the key to the bottomless pit. He seizes Satan and seals him in the bottomless pit for a thousand years. This thousand-year period coincides with the Reign of Christ on the earth.

When the thousand years are finished Satan is let loose for a short period. There is no specific time given, but he goes to the four corners of the earth to do what he has done since the Garden of Eden. He deceives those who have not accepted Christ as King in their hearts and gathers them together to attack the Holy City. Gog and Magog are specifically mentioned and much has been conjectured on who they might be. On that topic, may I remind you of the final 10 kingdoms (Rev. 17:12) which are not kingdoms we are familiar with at all? These are new kingdoms that reign with the Beast for a short time and are then utterly destroyed.

When Satan and his armies have gathered around the "camp of the saints," fire come down from God out of heaven and completely devours them all. The devil is seized again and this time is thrown into the eternal lake of fire where the beast and false prophet are. These three never face an opportunity to stand before the Great White Throne, but they are tormented day and night for ever and ever (Revelation 20:7-8)

**The Great White Throne**

It is at this time that the Eternal Christ mounts the Throne of Heaven and sits to judge all of the dead (Rev. 20:11-15). It is important to note that this judgment throne is for the dead. Four times it mentions in two verses that it is the dead who are to be judged. The righteous have been given eternal life, they will not be standing for judgment at this throne.

The earth and heaven have fled away from the presence of this throne. I believe the prophecy in II Peter 3:10 which states that the elements will melt with a fervent heat is what happens here.

This is that "Day of the Lord."

The dead, small and great will stand before this Throne and be judged out of the book of life and all of the books which record their deeds and the commands which they were given.

Everyone will be judged according to their works, and when they are not found in the book of life, they will be cast into the lake of fire along with the beast and false prophet. This judgment is on their eternal souls and as such will be eternal punishment. Jesus explains this clearly:

> *"And if thy foot offend thee, cut it off: it is better for thee to enter halt into life, than having two feet to be cast into hell, into the fire that never shall be quenched: Where their worm dieth not, and the fire is not quenched. And if thine eye offend thee, pluck it out: it is better for thee to enter into the kingdom of God with one eye, than having two eyes to be cast into hell fire: Where their worm dieth not, and the fire is not quenched."*
> *Mark 9:45-48*

In the Gospel of Luke Jesus describes the living torment that will be theirs:

> *"...And in hell he lift up his eyes, being in torments, and seeth Abraham afar off, and Lazarus in his bosom. And he cried and said, Father Abraham, have mercy on me, and send Lazarus, that he may dip the tip of his finger in water, and cool my tongue; for I am tormented in this flame. But Abraham said, Son, remember that thou in thy lifetime receivedst thy good things, and likewise Lazarus evil things: but now he is comforted, and thou art tormented... Then he said, I pray thee therefore, father, that thou wouldest send him to my father's house: For I have five brethren; that he may testify unto them, lest they also come into this place of torment. Abraham saith unto him, They have Moses and the prophets; let them hear them. And he said, Nay, father Abraham: but if one went unto them from the dead, they will repent. And he said unto him, If*

*they hear not Moses and the prophets, neither will they be per-*
*suaded, though one rose from the dead." Luke 16:22-31*

In the last chapter of Isaiah, we are told that when we live in the New Heaven and New earth we will worship before the Lord and we will go out and look upon the carcasses of the transgressors and see them in their judgement.

*"For as the new heavens and the new earth, which I will make, shall remain before me, saith the LORD, so shall your seed and your name remain. And it shall come to pass, that from one new moon to another, and from one sabbath to another, shall all flesh come to worship before me, saith the LORD. And they shall go forth, and look upon the carcases of the men that have transgressed against me: for their worm shall not die, neither shall their fire be quenched; and they shall be an abhorring un-to all flesh." Isaiah 66:22-24*

The thought of eternal damnation is horrific and should inspire all of us to spread the good news of the Gospel to every creature as we have been commanded.

If you are reading this and have not yet put your trust in Christ, I implore you to put this down and beg God for forgiveness and salvation. He said that if you would call on Him, he would hear you and save you, no matter what you have done.

*"That if thou shalt confess with thy mouth the Lord Jesus, and shalt believe in thine heart that God hath raised him from the dead, thou shalt be saved. For with the heart man believeth un-to righteousness; and with the mouth confession is made unto salvation. For the scripture saith, Whosoever believeth on him shall not be ashamed. For there is no difference between the Jew and the Greek: for the same Lord over all is rich unto all that call upon him. For whosoever shall call upon the name of the Lord shall be saved." Romans 10:9-13*

# Section 5

**Chapter:** Nine

**Title:** The New World

**Summary:** Here we find the descriptions that follow the phrase, "Behold, I make all things new." It will be a completely new world order made by God and shared with us.

**Study Outline:**

1.  The New Relationship

2.  The New Heaven and Earth

3.  The New City

# 9

# The New World

## The New Relationship

The idea of being one is introduced to us in the very first book of the Bible. The first verse of Genesis introduces us to a God who is one yet more than one. "Elohim" is both a singular and a plural word. This One God says *"Let us make man in our image, after our likeness."* The Genesis account goes on to tell us that He created male and female in His image. He then charged them with cleaving together and becoming "one flesh."

Almost 2,000 times in the scriptures the word "one" is used. Sometimes it is utilized for numerical purposes and sometimes as a measure of separation from a group, but many times it is for some kind of unity. One such use is found in John 17 at the Last Supper. Jesus is giving His disciples their final instructions before He goes to the cross. As He completes the lessons, His face turns to heaven and He begins to talk to the Father. The prayer is moving and powerful, and our particular interest at this point is found near the end where He says these words:

*"Neither pray I for these alone, but for them also which shall believe on me through their word; **That they all may be one**; as thou, Father, art in me, and I in thee, **that they also may be one in us**: that the world may believe that thou hast sent me. And the glory which thou gavest me I have given them; **that they may be***

*one, **even as we are one**: I in them, and thou in me, that they **may be made perfect in one**; and that the world may know that thou hast sent me, and hast loved them, as thou hast loved me. Father, I will that they also, whom thou hast given me, be with me where I am; that they may behold my glory, which thou hast given me: for thou lovedst me before the foundation of the world." John 17:20-24*

Four times in these verses Jesus makes the statement that He desires for us to be one with Him and the Father as they are One. Searching the scriptures for clues to what this might mean, we come across the apostle Paul's comment on this very subject in Ephesians:

*"Husbands, love your wives, even as Christ also loved the church, and gave himself for it; That he might sanctify and cleanse it with the washing of water by the word, That he might present it to himself a glorious church, not having spot, or wrinkle, or any such thing; but that it should be holy and without blemish. So ought men to love their wives as their own bodies. He that loveth his wife loveth himself. For no man ever yet hated his own flesh; but nourisheth and cherisheth it, even as the Lord the church: For we are members of his body, of his flesh, and of his bones. or this cause shall a man leave his father and mother, and shall be joined unto his wife, **and they two shall be one flesh**. **This is a great mystery: but I speak concerning Christ and the church**." Ephesians 5:25-32*

The relationship of a husband and wife and their "oneness" is apparently a picture of the relationship between Christ and His church. The church is referred to as the Bride of Christ. You will find references to the "Marriage Supper." In Revelation 19:7 we are told that "His wife hath made herself ready." The New Jerusalem is prepared as a "bride for her husband," and she is called "the bride, the Lambs wife." Throughout the scriptures, there is an anticipation of a relationship with God that is eternal and pure. These last two chapters of Revelation define this relationship and bring all of the allusions to a head in one glorious description.

I am aware that some would have us believe that the Bride of Christ is only the local church or a gathering of local churches in the kingdom. They could not be further from the truth. The Bride includes all believers from the beginning of the story to the end. This relationship has been planned since before the world began (Ephesians 3:9-11). Even believing Israel is called "the church in the wilderness" (Acts 7:38), and Hebrews (4:2) states that they received the gospel as well.

This relationship is about eternity where all of the former things are passed away. This is the place to which all prophecy, all hope, all joy, and all inheritance are pointing.

On a side note– this relationship with Christ is the ultimate relationship. Marriage is only a picture of the true place of oneness and fellowship with our Creator. This is the main reason why adultery and fornication are considered to be such heinous crimes.

I believe that the Millennium (1000-year reign of Christ on earth) is the Marriage supper. See these passages for more on the subject: Luke 14:16; Revelation 19:9,17.

The Marriage Ceremony takes place between Revelation 21:2 and Revelation 21:9. Notice the difference in the description of the Bride:

> *"...prepared as a bride adorned for her husband." vs. 2*

> *"...I will shew thee the bride, the Lamb's wife." vs. 9*

Verse two shows us the entrance of the adorned bride at the end of the aisle. She has prepared herself in a white wedding gown (Rev. 19:7-8) and is now ready to meet her Groom. Verse nine describes her still as the bride, but now she is the wife, indicating that the ceremony is over.

A closer look at what happens between verses two and nine reveals the elements of a wedding ceremony. Notice the following:

- The Groom pledges to live with her   vs. 3

- The Groom guarantees her protection vs. 4

- The Groom signs the wedding certificate  vs. 5

- The Groom gives His name "I AM"  vs. 6 An interesting side note -He calls Himself the Alpha and Omega. When these two letters  αω  are placed together they form the Greek word "I breathe."

- The Groom promises to support her with His goods  vs. 6-7

- The Groom turns from all others and cleaves only to her  vs.8

Thus begins our eternal marriage with our Creator. Never again will we deal with the sin and evil that we currently find ourselves surrounded by. The prophet Isaiah indicates that we will be able to see those who have been cast into the lake of fire and that for all of eternity we will consider it.

> *"For as the new heavens and the new earth, which I will make, shall remain before me, saith the LORD, so shall your seed and your name remain. And it shall come to pass, that from one new moon to another, and from one sabbath to another, shall all flesh come to worship before me, saith the LORD. And they shall go forth, and look upon the carcases of the men that have transgressed against me: for their worm shall not die, neither shall their fire be quenched; and they shall be an abhorring unto all flesh." Isaiah 66:22-24*

**The New Heaven and Earth**

Revelation 20:11 states that the earth and heaven as we know it will flee from the face of the Great Judge, and then Revelation 21:1 goes on to explain that there will be a new heaven and a new earth. I believe this is an important truth that bears consideration. Religious lore has us living on clouds or planets. Some would even have us believe that the current world we live in will continue and that we will be in some form of spiritual dimension that overlaps it. However, the scriptures specifically state that the Old heaven and the old earth will pass away and that God has a completely new heaven and earth on which we are to live. There are descriptions given to help us understand this new place and it's differences from what we now know. Before we point out those differences its important to go back to Genesis and identify the creation of the earth and heaven we are familiar with.

The original Creation

- The Earth was completely covered in water   Gen. 1:2

- God brought light to the darkness before he created the sun, moon, and stars.  Gen. 1:3-5

- God separated the waters and made a firmament of air beneath the waters above and the waters beneath. Gen. 1:6-7

- God called this firmament of air "heaven." Gen. 1:8

- God separated the sea from the land. Gen. 1:9-10

- God made the plants grow from the ground. Gen. 1:1-13

- God created lights to be in the firmament. The sun, moon, and stars were placed between the waters above and the waters beneath. This would mean that there is a water canopy on the outside of the Universe and that the earth is the center of the cosmos. Gen. 1:14-19

- God created the fish and fowl to live in the water and in the air under the water.  Gen. 1:21-22

- God made the animals and man live on the land, and he made man have dominion over every living thing that was in the sea, air, and land. Gen. 1:24-31

As we know, sin came into the world and caused the entire creation to be damaged. The first judgment on the creation came in Genesis 6 with the advent of the worldwide flood. This was not a local flood, but one that encompassed the entire earth. Dr. Schofield and others have suggested that the water canopy ("waters which were above the firmament") collapsed at the time of the flood and this was the reason for the worldwide deluge. However, that would have been impossible because the water would have had to pass the sun, moon, and stars to get to the earth. I don't agree with Dr. Schofield on this.

The actual description of where the water came from is interesting. Genesis tells us that "the fountains of the great deep were broken up, and the windows of heaven were opened." The "great deep" would be the water under the earth. Heaven is described as the place between the waters. Opening the windows of heaven produced rain, which is what we experience today. It does not necessarily mean the dumping of water on us from outside the cosmos.

*"In the six hundredth year of Noah's life, in the second month, the seventeenth day of the month, the same day were all the fountains of the great deep broken up, and the windows of heaven were opened." Genesis 7:11*

When the flood subsided, God placed a bow in the cloud to testify of His everlasting covenant with man that He would never again curse the earth with a flood. The flood became a picture of the judgment on the world by the Word of God. Jesus said that we were "condemned already." The Word is what He said would judge us. Ephesians mentions a washing of water by the Word, identifying the water as the Word. This explains the John 3:5 reference to being "born of water."

Paul says in Roman chapter eight that the entire creation is still groaning and waiting for redemption. Struggling under the condemnation of the Word, the world looks for its Creator to redeem it. The redemption of the Creation comes in the form of fire to purge it according to Peter:

*"But the day of the Lord will come as a thief in the night; in the which the heavens shall pass away with a great noise, and the elements shall melt with fervent heat, the earth also and the*

This is when the earth and heaven will flee away from the face of the One who sits on the Great White Throne (Rev. 20:11).

After the first heaven and earth are passed away John writes that he saw a new heaven and new earth (Rev. 21:1). He is very specific about the fact that there is no more sea. The abyss of Genesis 1:2 is no more. The bottomless pit under which is kept the evil hoards in chains is gone. The water barrier is no more.

Mountains are still there according to Revelation 21:10. A great and high mountain is described as being in a place where the New City can be viewed in all of its glory.

There is no need for the sun or moon (Rev. 21:23) because the new city is the light of the world. The light of the city comes from the presence of the Lamb.

There are nations and kings on this new earth (Rev. 21:24). This is one of those things that is left without an explanation. Where do the nations come from? Where do the kings come from? Are there still children born and families created in this new world? There is no comment about this. We are left to wonder.

There is no more curse in this new world (Rev. 22:3), but there is a tree whose leaves give healing to the nations. Why do they need to be healed? I don't know.

Another interesting thing about this tree of life is that it has twelve different kinds of fruits and yields a different fruit each month. This indicates that there is a passing of time even though time is declared to be no more (Rev. 22:2). I'm not sure what all that means, but I am convinced that this place will be an interesting place.

**The New City**

The New Jerusalem is described as the bride of Christ and it is the city where the saints will live. This city will be on the new heaven and new earth and it has some unique features that we need to look into. Revelation 21-22:

- It seems to be a pre-fab construction because it descends in its entirety out of heaven from God (Rev. 21:10). Wow! Just think about the construction that is now taking place! Just think of the place that has been prepared for you (John 14:2-3)

- Its overall color and brilliance "like a jasper stone, clear as crystal" will also be enough light to fill the earth and heaven. (Rev. 21:23;22:5)

- The city itself is "foursquare." We would call that cubed. The width, length, and height are equal. 12,000 furlongs would come out to somewhere around 1500 miles. So it would be 1500 miles long, 1500 miles wide, and 1500 miles tall. At its base, it would be about 2,250,00 square miles (larger than India). Giving each story a generous 12 feet, it would be over 600,000 stories tall. If you were 5,000 miles away from the city it would still appear to be 130 times larger than the moon.

- It has a great wall around it with twelve gates. Each gate is a pearl. (Pearls are made by suffering. Jesus said that He is the door. John 10:9). On the names of the gates are the twelve tribes of Israel, indicating that they also have part of this city (Romans 3:1-2). The gates are always open (Rev. 21:25), indicating complete freedom of movement. There appear to be constant comings and goings (Rev. 2:24-27).

- The size of the wall is given to us in cubits, but the cubits, which would normally be about 18 inches based on the length of a man's forearm, are stated as being according to the measure of the angel. We have no idea how big he was. Based on a human cubit the wall around the city would be about 216 feet tall.

- There are twelve foundations under the wall of the city. In those twelve foundations are the names of the twelve apostles. The twelve foundations are garnished with precious stones.

They are as follows:

**Jasper-** Usually red, yellow, brown, or green in color; and sometimes blue

**Sapphire-** Typically blue, but some sapphires also occur in yellow, purple, orange, and green colors

**Chalcedony-** Commonly seen in white to gray, can be seen in grayish-blue or various shades of brown ranging from pale to nearly black

**Emerald-** Green

**Sardonyx-** A variant of onyx in which the colored bands are varying shades of red

**Sardius-** Mostly red ranging from pale orange to an intense almost-black color

**Chrysolite-** Green, olive. The word itself means "gold stone"

**Beryl-** Pure beryl is colorless but sometimes it will be tinted by various colors based on the mineral mixed in with it.

**Topaz-** Usually identified as golden yellow and blue, it comes in a variety of colors, including colorless. The rarest are natural pinks, reds, and delicate golden oranges, sometimes with pink hues.

**Chrysoprasus-** normally apple-green, but can be varying degrees of green

**Jacinth-** dark blue

**Amethyst-** a purple variety of quartz

- There is no temple in this city because the Lord God Almighty and the Lamb are the temple of it. (Rev. 21:22

- Only those who are written in the Lamb's book of life are welcome in this city. (Psalm 139)

- There is a pure river of the water of life that flows from the throne of God and of the Lamb (Rev. 22:1). This river is free to drink from (Rev. 22:17).

- The street of the city is pure gold and looks like transparent glass. (Rev. 21:21) Down the middle of the street and on either side of the street is the tree of life. This tree yields 12 different kinds of fruit. A different one each month.

- We will be able to see the face of the Lamb. (Rev. 22:3)

- There are nations and families in this city. (Mathew 8:11, Revelation 21:24).


What a beautiful place to live!

**Chapter:** Ten

**Title:** Epilogue

**Summary:** This is the final wrap-up of the message. It places a period not only on the book of Revelation but also on the entire Bible.


**Study Outline:**

1. The Open Seal
2. The Signature
3. The Post Script

# 10

# Epilogue

**The Open Seal**

As the story comes to a close we see John falling at his feet to worship the angel who brought the message. The angel is very clear that he is not to be worshipped (Rev. 22:8-9), and states that he is a fellow servant of John. This statement is reminiscent of the admonition of Paul in Colossians, which cautions us about the voluntary worship of angels.

*"Let no man beguile you of your reward in a voluntary humility and worshipping of angels, intruding into those things which he hath not seen, vainly puffed up by his fleshly mind," Col. 2:18*

There are over 800 references in the Bible dealing with angels and their interactions with mankind. They are no doubt a part of the whole story, but it is important to remember that they are servants of the Almighty as are we.

The angel goes on to tell John not to seal up the book because this book is for the saints to read and understand. This is different than what Isaiah and Daniel were told:

*"Bind up the testimony, seal the law among my disciples." Isaiah 8:16*

*"And I heard, but I understood not: then said I, O my Lord, what shall be the end of these things? And he said, Go thy way,*

*Daniel: for the words are closed up and sealed till the time of the end." Daniel 12:8-9*

The angels' instructions are more in line with what Jesus said when he was explaining things to his disciples in Matthew. His comment was to those who would read the scriptures as opposed to those who were listening to Him at that time:

*"When ye therefore shall see the abomination of desolation, spoken of by Daniel the prophet, stand in the holy place, **(whoso readeth, let him understand**:)" Matthew 24:15*

## The Signature

As with any letter, there is always a signature at the end. We are given the Lord's signature in very clear terms. Each Person of the Trinity signs the letter. First He states that He is Alpha and Omega, the beginning and the End. This is the signature of the Father:

*"And, behold, I come quickly; and my reward is with me, to give every man according as his work shall be. **I am Alpha and Omega, the beginning and the end, the first and the last**." Revelation 22:12-13*

Next, the Son of God puts His name and credentials on the line:

*"**I Jesus** have sent mine angel to testify unto you these things in the churches. **I am the root and the offspring of David, and the bright and morning star**." Revelation 22:16*

Finally, we hear the voice of the Spirit:

*"**And the Spirit and the bride say, Come**. And let him that heareth say, Come. And let him that is athirst come. And whosoever will, let him take the water of life freely." Revelation 22:17*

## The Postscript

The final statement of the book is a warning to those who will tamper with the message. Adding to the Word will bring chastening on the one who does. This chastening is most likely something that happens in this life. Those who would add additional books to the testimony and additional revelations will be plagued by the same plagues that are written in the book. I believe this is a reference not only to Revelation itself but also to the rest of the scriptures.

*"For I testify unto every man that heareth the words of the prophecy of this book, If any man shall add unto these things, God shall add unto him the plagues that are written in this book:" Revelation 22:18*

The second warning is to those who will remove things from the book. This condemnation is an eternal one. It states that those who take away from the words of the book will be removed from the book of life (Revelation 20:15), and will not take part in any of the events in the holy city, nor from the blessings in the book. Translators and Bible publishing companies should take note.

*"And if any man shall take away from the words of the book of this prophecy, God shall take away his part out of the book of life, and out of the holy city, and from the things which are written in this book." Revelation 22:19*